Greenwich Council
Library & Information Service

IN HOUSE
QUALITY
SYSTEMS

Woolwich Library
Calderwood Street, SE18 6QZ
020 8921 5750

RE

Please return by the last date shown

WO 30/07/08

Thank
You!

To renew, please contact any Greenwich library

Issue: 02   Issue Date: 06.06.00   Ref: RM.RBL.LIS

Letters to my Golf Club

www.rbooks.co.uk

'The least thing upset him on the links. He missed short putts because of the uproar of the butterflies in the adjoining meadows.'

P.G. Wodehouse

Letters to my Golf Club

DOM JOLY

BANTAM PRESS

LONDON · TORONTO · SYDNEY · AUCKLAND · JOHANNESBURG

TRANSWORLD PUBLISHERS
61–63 Uxbridge Road, London W5 5SA
A Random House Group Company
www.rbooks.co.uk

First published in Great Britain
in 2007 by Bantam Press
an imprint of Transworld Publishers

Copyright © Dom Joly 2007

With the exception of the Lindsay-Bird characters, who are completely fictional, in all cases names of people have been changed or omitted entirely and the locations and addresses of golf clubs have been removed, changed and relocated to protect the privacy of others.

Dom Joly has asserted his right under the Copyright, Designs and Patents Act 1988 to be identified as the author of this work.

A CIP catalogue record for this book
is available from the British Library.

ISBN 9780593058770

Addresses for Random House Group Ltd companies outside the UK
can be found at: www.randomhouse.co.uk
The Random House Group Ltd Reg. No. 954009

The Random House Group Ltd makes every effort to ensure that the papers used in its books are made
from trees that have been legally sourced from well-managed and credibly certified forests. Our paper
procurement policy can be found at: www.randomhouse.co.uk/paper.htm

Printed and bound in Great Britain by
Butler & Tanner, Frome, Somerset

2 4 6 8 10 9 7 5 3 1

INTRODUCTION

I was playing a round of golf with Simon Kelner, editor of the *Independent*, when the idea came to me. Simon has a much-loved dog called Rovi, whom he often brings with him. He's a small dog and very well behaved. Someone, however, disagreed. Simon told me that a member of the club had written a letter to complain that Rovi had put them off their game. I couldn't believe that this could be the case. I also couldn't believe that anyone had bothered to write in about it. Then it hit me. Not a golf ball – the idea for this book. Here's the result.

I'm a rubbish golfer. I avoided the game like the plague for years. It was just a bit … naff. My dad is a very keen golfer and this had put me off quite early on in life. However, middle age, moving to the Cotswolds, and a weekend in Marrakesh with Piers Morgan (it's a long story, which involves the daughter of the King of Morocco's being struck with a golf ball after one of my appalling drives) made me determined to take up the game properly. Weirdly, golf seems to have had a bit of a revival and is now almost cool. I hope that this book will be the answer for the thousands of non-golfers who have to give a golfing relative or friend a present and are tired of buying 'novelty' balls or pairs of socks. That's my cynical, commercial aim, anyway. I do actually enjoy playing golf. Obviously it helps if I'm somewhere tropical by the sea, but it's good fun. I hate the whole 'my life is a golf club' thing and I'm not that keen on the clothes, but it now gives me another activity to do when I'm on holiday, and that can only be good.

I've always loved letters books – from the seminal Henry Root oeuvre to *Letters from a Nut* to the brilliant *Timewaster* series. The irony is that I'm a terrible letter writer and never get round to it. I prefer the immediacy of emails. There is, however, something special about letters and I'm so glad that I managed to find people who still write them.

I'd like to thank everyone who unwittingly became involved in my scam. You were all incredibly patient, considering the nonsense I was writing. I have endeavoured to anonymise your replies out of respect. Some people didn't humour me at all. I failed to get replies from quite a few efforts, including letters soliciting interest in a new type of golf cart. I have included some of these letters at the back of the book, to show that it's not quite as easy a job as it might look.

I started writing the letters just over a year ago. As I wrote, I created a whole fictional family of complainers:

Colonel Arthur J. Lindsay-Bird: a crusty, battle-scarred old Tory, with a dodgy military past that has clearly left him a touch unhinged. He has just lost his beloved Danish chicken hound (this type of dog does actually exist – look it up) and there is the hint of a feeling that the letters are some kind of desperate cry for help.

His wife, Julia: clearly a deeply unhappy and very short woman who has put up with the Colonel for a little bit too long. There are hints that Julia was once a model and lived a more glamorous life than in the present. It also seems that she might have inherited quite a lot of money, unfortunately now squandered by the Colonel.

Son Dave, or David: a television producer, working for Mental Productions (surely a little clue?), and a hybrid of many people I have come across in the world of television. Think Nathan Barley meets Normski. Dave, for some unaccountable reason, is black.

Son Randy: gay, and very much into golf like his father, the Colonel. He runs the Tight Hole Society and doesn't seem to see eye to eye with his father.

There is, possibly, between Dave and Randy, a hybrid son that the Colonel might get on with. Sadly, family is not that easy. Between them, the Lindsay-Birds have postally harassed golf courses all around the UK and beyond for the last year.

It's weird writing a book like this because it is very much out of your control. You send off a ream of letters and then sit and wait for the replies to come in. It did make the postman's daily arrival a great excitement. If I got a reply to one of my letters it was all very thrilling and I would fire off a riposte and sit down to wait again. There were times when I had no responses for a month and it would get very depressing. Then, suddenly, I'd get a deluge. I did get a bit paranoid at one stage that clubs had been warned off me by some sort of efficient inter-golf-course communication network. Happily this didn't seem to be the case. I found that I had the most replies from Ireland. The most trusting correspondence came from Scotland, and the most aggressive from England. Wales seemed bemused by the whole thing. I have also learned a little more than I previously knew about Denmark. It sounds great and, should things in my life go pear-shaped, I shall be paying a visit.

I hope you enjoy the book.

Dom Joly

P.S Please note that while names and addresses have been altered or obscured to protect the innocent, every single letter from a golf club in this book is a completely genuine response to a Lindsay-Bird letter.

ACKNOWLEDGMENTS

Finally, I'd like to thank everyone who helped me make this book happen:
My wife, Stacey, for designing all the letters, and putting up with me constantly
demanding that she print off more at three in the morning.
Al Campbell for his amazing illustrations.
Jonny Geller and Doug Kean at Curtis Brown.
And everyone at Transworld for their faith in the project.

QUEENS GATE
SCHOOL ROAD, CIRENCESTER
GLOUCESTERSHIRE,
GLX 6DU

The Club Secretary
Chipsbury Golf Club
Tungsten Green

21st June 2006

Dear Sir or Madam,

I write to you about a rather distressing personal matter in which I hope you might be able to help. I am a long suffering wife whose husband is, to put it bluntly, a total bastard and having an affair.

He met the current ceiling watcher that he's running around with at an arms fair in Rotterdam. He swept her off her feet with all sorts of bollocks about his war "experiences" I believe that he's now been playing "Mr Wobbly hides his helmet" with her for just over a year now but he denies it point blank whenever I confront him.

What on earth has this got to do with us I hear you cry? I'll tell you. My husband does not play golf and yet I have now found at least seven receipts from your golf club in his trouser pockets.

I want to know what's going on? He doesn't play golf so are you simply allowing people to "check in" to your establishment under the pretext of playing golf and then allowing them to fornicate willy-nilly on your premises? If so then this is a disgrace and I intend to notify the appropriate authorities. My father was a golfer and I've always been under the impression that golf clubs were respectable places not bordellos where some blonde bosom-bank can take my husband for a spot of this and that?

If you are genuinely unaware of this situation then I demand that you investigate and close off any rooms that could be used for jiggly to non-married customers. I would also demand that you refuse accommodation, entry or any service to an Arthur Lindsay-Bird the next time he attempts to use your premises. It's just not on. He might attempt to use his "Aden" name of "Colonel Hoo-Ha". He was mutilated over there so he's not exactly forgettable.

Do not make me have to come and pay a visit to your establishment.

Yours truly,

Julia.S.Lindsay-Bird (Mrs)

CHIPSBURY GOLF CLUB

Tungsten Green

Mrs Julia Lindsay-Bird
Queens Gate
School Road
Cirencester
Gloucestershire
GLX 6DU

23 June 2006

Dear Mrs Lindsay Bird

In reply to your letter dated 21 June I think you may have the wrong golf club.

We have been trying for over 4 years to obtain planning permission for a hotel on the golf course without success so we are not the bordellos you thought we were!

I am sorry to hear of your predicament, but what I can say is that Arthur, from your point of view, looks to have reached his 'sell by date'.

It would appear that you would not need to pay a visit to this establishment unless you have thoughts on taking up golf.

I will however look out for any blond bosom-bank with male companion.

The Club Secretary
Chipsbury Golf Club
Tungsten Green

27th June 2006

Dear Mr ████

May I just start by thanking you for your kind reply to my letter of the 21st of June? In a small way you've rekindled my faith in the essential goodness of "the golfer" as a human specimen. It's good to know that you're not all heartless cheating bastards.

You sound like a good man, not unlike my late father. He was a wonderful man who, although racked with guilt about the whole "Kirtlington Affair" that I'm sure you remember was all over the papers. I was always of the view that he could never have done what he was accused of but then, he was my father, so what else could I think? He was always adamant that I shouldn't marry Arthur. I think he felt that he wasn't the right sort to run the brewery. He was spot on of course. Arthur took it over when my father passed on and drove it into the ground before selling it off for several million less than its actual worth. Then he went and set up his current business of "security" for westerners in the Middle East. Apparently the desert was in his blood.

But I digress. I don't have anyone to talk to about all of this so forgive me. There's something so cathartic about a letter, don't you think? It's such a shame that our lives today are so blighted by email and telephones. When I was modelling I'd get sent one letter telling me where to go and what the job was and that was that. I've never ever used a portable telephone even on foreign locations.

Back to my original letter- I was never insinuating that you might actually have a hotel on your premises (I imagine no member's marriage would last if that were the case). It's just that I'm certain that Arthur has been to your club at least half a dozen times with this voracious Jezebel and he wasn't playing golf so…it doesn't take a rocket scientist…

I shall leave you alone. Actually that's pretty much all I feel at the moment- alone. I get so angry when I think of all the time that I've wasted on that burn-scarred bastard. Yet, I do still love him, he needs me I think. I do thank you for listening and beg you to just let me know from your records when and how often he has been to your club in the last six months?

Yours sincerely,

Julia B

Julia.S.Lindsay-Bird (Mrs)

NO REPLY

QUEENS GATE
SCHOOL ROAD, CIRENCESTER
GLOUCESTERSHIRE,
GLX 6DU

The Club Secretary,
Three Ways Golf Club,
Whittle-on-the-Wold,
Oxfordshire,
OX23 0NQ

21st June 2006

Dear Sir,

I'm afraid to say that I've played my first and my very last round of golf at your club. Allow me to explain: I've always been in two minds as to whether animals of any kind should be allowed on the golf turf. I recently worked in Dubai where my nearest course allowed a motley collection of wild dogs, stray cats, desert coyotes and even the odd camel to wander about wherever they felt like. I have to admit to occasionally swinging a well-aimed drive at a beast or two but it was an uphill struggle. Particularly curious since the Arabs are such animal haters but there you go, that's Johnny Foreigner for you.

Anyway, I digress. I was playing an enjoyable round on your course and had just reached the eighth hole when the trouble began. I was addressing my ball on the tee when I was distracted by the sound of yapping and enthusiastic clapping and cheering from a small crowd of people behind a clump of nearby trees. I un-adressed my ball and went over to see what the commotion was and to ask them to desist.

The scene I came upon still resonates vividly in my mind. Two burly looking men with shaven heads were urging on a couple of terrier-like dogs that were ripping each other apart in a particularly violent manner. There were about five other people in regular golfing attire who seemed to be enjoying this dog-fight (for this is clearly what it was) and egging the poor beasts on.

Being an ex-military man I attempted to intervene and separate the dogs. At this juncture one of the burly men punched me in the Solar Plexus and told me to "f**k off before I f***ing kick your arse." I asked them whether they were anything to do with the golf club and they informed me that they were "all f***ing members, and who the f**k are you f**k-face?" Sensing excessive impending violence and worried that I would not be able to control myself (I am ex-Special Forces by the by) I retreated to my Morgan and drove away from the course without informing anyone.

I now regret my actions and wish that I had approached someone and made a formal complaint. I wish to be assured that these "gentlemen" were not members of your club and that you do not condone dog fighting on your premises? I await your response.

Yours sincerely

Colonel Arthur.J.Lindsay-Bird (ret)

THREE WAYS GOLF CLUB

Three Ways Golf Club
Whittle-on-the-Wold, Oxfordshire,
OX23 0NQ

Colonel A J Lindsay-Bird
Queens Gate
School Road
Cirencester
Gloucestershire
GLX 6DU

24 June 2006

Dear Sir,

I am in receipt of your letter of 21st June, received yesterday, and can only express my deepest regrets for the experiences that you suffered on your recent visit to ~~████████████~~ I have tried to find a telephone contact for you without success, hence the need for this letter.

I can only say that in my 20 ish years as Club Secretary, I have never heard of such an incident taking place, and therefore need your assistance in bringing this matter to a very speedy conclusion.

What would most useful, if you can let me know details of the occurrence, and through our Tee checking in system, we may be able to identify the offenders and deal with them in an appropriate manner. At the moment, from the little information your have detailed, it is too early to say as to whether or not they are Members of ~~████████~~ GC, and if so will not be for much longer. If it is determined that were visitors, I can assure you that they will not be welcome at our Club again in the future.

Could you please therefore let us know the following, to assist us in our enquiries:

The date of the occurrence, your Tee Time, and person in whose name the Tee booking was made, whether or not the group to whom you refer were playing ahead or behind your group, and anything other information that you feel is appropriate.

If instead you would like to telephone me any evening at home after 6.30pm, I would be pleased to receive any information that can be used to find the offenders at the earliest.

I have already discussed your letter with the Club Captain and Vice Captain, and will also be discussing with the Directors. Please be assured that we not rest until this matter in concluded.

QUEENS GATE
SCHOOL ROAD, CIRENCESTER
GLOUCESTERSHIRE,
GLX 6DU

The Club Secretary,
Three Ways Golf Club,
Whittle-on-the-Wold,
Oxfordshire,
OX23 0NQ

27th June 2006

Dear Sir,

Thank you for your letter of the 24th June in reply to my letter of the 21st of June regarding the dog-fighting incident on your course. I am glad to hear that you are as shocked as I am by the whole affair and intend to do something about it. It had crossed my mind that perhaps I might be the only person who found this sort of thing offensive. Thank God this does not appear to be the case. There's already too much abnormal behaviour in this country of ours for my liking.

As to your queries- I think that the golfers must have been playing ahead of me, as I did not see them until I came across the "event". One of them was wearing a blue golf sweater and another had very bright white shoes. Although trained to notice such detail in the Forces I'm afraid that Times' Winged Chariot has taken a bit of a toll on the old grey matter. I was involved in the Wadi Kbir uprising in Aden and was severely wounded for my efforts, so bear with me.

The two shaven headed men who seemed to be running the bloodbath were both wearing black leather jackets, denim jeans and were, from their accents, Cockneys. If I had to make a guess I would venture that they might be taxi drivers, but I stress that this is based on personal instinct and not fact.

As far as I remember the round was booked in Julia, my wife's name although I could be mistaken. I'm afraid that I'm very bad with time and dates but to the best of my recollection this would have been about eleven am on either the fourth or the fifth of February 1994. I remember this because my wife's birthday is on the 28th and it was around then.

I do hope this will help you in your enquiries. If you have any other questions then please contact me. I am not surprised that you were unable to contact me on the telephone as I do not possess one. I personally believe that they are the instrument of Satan and will never allow one, portable or otherwise in my house.

Yours sincerely,

NO REPLY

Colonel Arthur.J.Lindsay-Bird (ret)

MENTAL productions

...Gate, School Road, Cirencester
...ucestershire, GLX 6DU

4th July 2006

Sir,

I'm Dave Lindsay-Bird, Senior Development Producer at Mental Productions. You probably know about Mental already. We were responsible for the award-winning series: "Pimpolympics" on Bravo hosted by the legendary Snoop Doggy-Dog. Following the phenomenal success of that series State-side, the Channel is keen for us to come up with a "vehicle" for Snoop to do here in the UK. That's where you come in.

We need a location of a beautiful golf course for a day's filming sometime next month. The idea is simple and it came straight from Da Snoop. It's called "Golf on Drugs." The premise is a fun/educational one- just how bad for your co-ordination and concentration are various types of stimulants and narcotics? We go from the legal- Guarana, coffee, vodka to the illegal end of the spectrum with Meth-Amphetamine, LSD and Marijuana. Obviously this has all been pre-cleared with the relevant authorities. It's actually a sort of medical programme in a way. We'll have professional doctors on location to check the amounts and the progress of Snoop and his "crew".

The day would be broken down into two parts:

The morning- Snoop and da Crew arrive, do some chillin' and then play a couple of normal rounds of golf whilst being filmed (Snoop is an accomplished golfer and won the Celebrity pro-am in Vegas in 2005).

The afternoon- Snoop and da Crew consume each designated narcotic under close medical supervision and then attempt to play another round of golf.

At the end of the day we can look at their scores and interview them to see how each substance affected their game. I've approached Jamie Theakston about presenting and I'm sure that this is a goer. I think that we can make this one of the most talked about series of this year. It'll be great publicity for your club and, obviously there's a sizeable location fee that we need to discuss. I don't expect you guys to do this for free. Can you write me with a ballpark figure?

Golf on!

Dave!

Dave Lindsay-Bird

Eagle Country Club

Mr Dave Lindsay-Bird
Senior Development Producer
Mental Productions
Queens Gate
School Road
Cirencester
Gloucestershire
GLX 6DU

12 July 2006

Dear Mr Lindsay-Bird

Golf on Drugs, Filming

Thank you very much for your letter of 4July. We were pleased to be considered as possible location for the project. However, after some discussion I regret that it was decided we cannot accept the inevitable disruption that our experience indicates filming would incur.

Our courses are extremely busy for the weeks ahead particularly as, in addition to the usual volume of golf tourists and members on holiday, we hold an open tournament in early August.

I hope you can find an alternative as your project sound worthwhile.

Yours sincerely

Sir,   15th July 2006

Thank you for your letter dated the 12th of July in response to my original letter dated the 4th of July re the proposal to use your golf course as a location for "Golf On Drugs." I was saddened to note that you felt that you would not be able to approve the use of your beautiful course especially as you note that the whole "project sounds worthwhile."

Now as you might have ascertained from my first letter, golf is not really my sport. When I first took this project on I was taken aside for a quiet drink and warned by a couple of old golf-hands that I might face some hostility to this project because of the ethnicity of the presenter, Snoop Doggy-Dog.

Reading between the lines of your letter I'm picking up a problem with the fact that Snoop is black. I know that the golf world is a very "laundered" environment and I totally respect your wish to keep it that way. Personally I really felt that Snoop would be ideal for this project with his obvious expertise in both fields. However, this is television and we don't deal in ideals, we deal in getting stuff on the telly and Jim, I need to get this project on the telly or my arse is on the street.

So, what I propose is that we swap presenters for the project for something we're already doing with Joe Pasquale. Joe, a keen golfer himself and obviously white (pasty to be honest, between you and me, he's not well), could take on the presenting role for "Golf On Drugs." Da Snoop could take over Joe's project- "Monkhunter with Tara Palmer Tompkinson." (This is a Da Vinci spin-off where Tara and now maybe Da Snoop hunt down Benedictine Monks in a ruined Irish monastery using paint-ball guns) it's for ITV 4 and they love it.

We really are keen to use your course so, if we made this simple ethnic compromise and offered say, twenty thousand pounds for the day's filming, surely we can play ball?

Look forward to hearing back from you ASAP as we need to get this show on the road.

Och Aye!

Dave!

Dave Lindsay-Bird
Senior Development Producer

Eagle Country Club

Mr Dave Lindsay-Bird
Senior Development Producer
Mental Productions
Queens Gate
School Road
Cirencester
Gloucestershire
GLX 6DU

18 July 2006

Dear Mr Lindsay-Bird

Golf on Drugs, Filming

I found your letter of 15 July extremely offensive and insulting to the Club and the game of golf. Until you raised the matter we had not contemplated in any manner the ethnicity of the presenter.

Our decision was taken purely on the potential disruption to play on the course given that this Club has a great proportion of tee times on the course reserved well ahead of time by members and visitors.

In the light of your letter we would not consider participating in any way now with your projects
Yours sincerely

MENTAL
productions

Queens Gate, School Road, Cirencester
Gloucestershire, GLX 6DU

24th July 2006

Jim,

Thank you for you extremely prompt reply to my last letter regarding the "Golf On Drugs" programme. I can only apologise for my insinuations re DaSnoop. It appears that I've completely got the wrong end of the stick. I now understand that your reasons for not wanting to be involved in the programme are due to your popularity and not to do with the fact that Da Snoop is a convicted black felon.

As a man of colour myself, I'm so glad to hear that ethnicity plays no sinister role in the world of golf, even behind the scenes. I can only applaud your multi-cultural outlook. I do totally understand that, given the circumstances, you now feel a tad uncomfortable with this particular project and wouldn't want to host it at your golf course. For your information we have agreed to use a golf course in Gloucestershire for "GoD" and Joe Pasquale was never even told about the potential swap from "Monkhunter" so nobody got hurt.

However, before I leave you alone and bearing in mind your enthusiasm for "Benetton" style TV, I wondered if I could just mention one other programme that we are developing here at Mental? It's a docu-drama based on the idea that golf is primarily a game of the mind. It's called "Could Bruce Lee Have Beaten Tiger Woods At Golf?" It's starring David Yip (Ex-Chinese Detective) as Bruce Lee and Danny from Hear'Say as Tiger Woods. It's for BBC3 and they're going to launch their Autumn season with it and you know how successful they've been so far. Once again we'd love to use your golf course as a location. The fee would be in the same ballpark as the previous one. Come on….you know you want to……

"I'd like to teach the world to sing, in perfect harmony."

Dave

Dave Lindsay-Bird
Senior Development Producer

Eagle Country Club

Mr Dave Lindsay-Bird
Senior Development Producer
Mental Productions
Queens Gate
School Road
Cirencester
Gloucestershire
GLX 6DU

04 August 2006

Dear Mr Lindsay-Bird

Golf Filming

Thank you very much for your reply to my letter and I accept you apology and consider that aspect closed.

You are approaching the Club at a bad time as we are in the midst of our competition season ~~and we have 200 players working for Sylvan competition and it will run until 30 September~~. However, what you are suggesting is of interest and I am not rejecting your project out of hand.

Finding time on our courses is and will be a problem for the remainder of this year, but and I make no promises at this time we will give due consideration to your proposal. I would like to request that you give me an outline of what you require, particularly in the length of time you envisage filming on the course will take, I will take it to my committee and do my best for you.

~~Royal Berkshire~~ would be a wonderful setting for you. I know from travel documentaries and other golf programmes that we are photogenic and you can check this out on ~~www.eagle.com~~ where there is a picture gallery.

Yours sincerely

Secretary/Manager

MENTAL
productions

Queens Gate, School Road, Cirencester
Gloucestershire, GLX 6DU

16th August 2006

Yo Jim,

Apologies for the delay in replying to your last letter dated the 4th of August. I have been away in Ireland overseeing the location shoot of "Monkhunter" starring the troubled media entity that is Tara Palmer-Tompkinson and presented, as previously discussed, by Joe Pasquale who, I promise you, is still completely unaware of the switch we nearly organised. The shoot was quite an ordeal, I can tell you, and I was forced to stay out there longer than planned after Tompkinson badly injured one of the monks with one of her homemade monk-traps. The whole monastery became very aggressive over the incident- quite surprising when you think that they're men of god. I guess the old adage- "never work with animals or children" must now, sadly, be amended to include Benedictine monks.

The good news is that I have been promoted from Senior Development Producer to Executive Development Producer here at Mental. This means I have a lot more power now so you're definitely talking to the right guy!! To business- I note with excitement your interest in the "Could Bruce Lee Have Beaten Tiger Woods At Golf?" project. As I told you we have secured the collective talents of Danny from Hear'Say and David Yip (The Chinese Detective) to star in this Asian/Infotainment/Fictionsport project for BBC3.

We would need some golf garb for The Tiger Woods character but Bruce Lee will be dressed very simply in a small orange thong and greased with toasted sesame oil (highlights the vein structure on camera). Tiger will also require a set of golf clubs but Bruce will be using nothing but a Numchukka and his mind.

As for the course, as long as nothing terrible happens we would need it for two days. The first day would be spent setting cameras in the dolly ditches and wiring up the aerial high-fives. We would also be setting down two belchers that I hope will not inconvenience too many people. The second day would be "lights, cameras, action!" We would film the two playing two full rounds of golf and "Robert est ton oncle" as they say in France.

I notice that the ████████████████ is a ██████ of the club. Do you think she might be persuaded, if we chuck a fistful of fivers towards a charity to go two rounds in the ring with Bruce Lee and his Numchukkas for the DVD extras? Just a thought.

"No woman no cry."

Dave!

Dave Lindsay-Bird
Executive Development Producer

Eagle Country Club

Mr Dave Lindsay-Bird
Senior Development Producer
Mental Productions
Queens Gate
School Road
Cirencester
Gloucestershire
GLX 6DU

21 August 2006

Dear Mr Lindsay-Bird

Golf Filming

Thank you very much for your letter of 16 August. I am sorry that your visit to the monastery appears to be a stressful time.

Happily, after the past 2 weeks, life here has returned to a more usual and comfortable pattern and we are pleased that the security issues at airports does not appear to have deterred too many golfers.

Appreciating that you would appreciate a quick response, I brought your letter to the attention of the Club's newly appointed Captain. He feels after some discussion with others on the committee that the disruption to play would be unacceptable to members and visitors, albeit that you are offering a fair and attractive fee.

I regret therefore that I have to reply that we will be unable to be a venue for your filming.

Yours sincerely

29th August 2006

Yo Jim,

Thank you so much for your letter of the 21st of August. I'm so glad that, after the recent security issues at the airports, things have returned to normal for you. You can get on with your life, hiking up and down glens, hunting Haggis, whatever. Not for me. Not for me, Jim . Here I am, working my black ass off to justify my recent promotion to Executive Development Producer and my very first project gets metaphorically told to go and sit at the back of the bus.

Maybe I'm just not cut out for the TV business? My parents hate it. They wanted me to go into the law (not the Babylon, the legal side) but TV's always had this magnetic appeal. From the moment that I saw the brother on Emmerdale, it's all I've ever really wanted to do.

I'm not waving but drowning here Jim . TV's a white man's world and I'm feeling blue. Back in February I went to see a head doctor and he put me on anti-depressants- 60mg a day. Somedays booze and horse are the only friends I have.

Have you ever failed at anything Jim ? I mean really failed. Like failed so bad that everyone in the company suddenly stops whispering about you when you come into the room on your skateboard? Have you ever woken up and, instead of feeling the first warm fingers of the sun caress your face, feel like sticking the cold hard steel of a Colt 45 down your throat? I have Jim , every goddam' morning of my life.

But I digress. TV's a lonely world Jim . It's a world where, if you show weakness you're ripped apart by the wolves. I'm no wolf Jim but I ain't no sheep neither. I'm more of a porcupine if pressed, prickly on the outside but soft and mushy on the inside like a Scotch Egg. I don't know why I'm laying all this on you man? I just feel like you're someone who understands me. I need a break from all this. What would you think if I just flew up there next weekend and we have a couple of whiskys and talk- talk like real men who are not afraid to cry. Let it all come out. It's been so long and I'm just so tired Jim - I'm just so goddam' tired. Let me know what day's good for you.

"Iron, like Lion, In Zion,"

Dave!

Dave Lindsay-Bird
Executive Development Producer

Eagle Country Club

~~Certificate/address line~~

Mr Dave Lindsay-Bird
Senior Development Producer
Mental Productions
Queens Gate
School Road
Cirencester
Gloucestershire
GLX 6DU

15 September 2006

Dear Dave

Sorry to read from your letter when I returned from business meetings in London that life is not a bed of roses for you. I can assure that the grass is not always green in a golf club ~~...~~

I am afraid your suggestion of flying ~~...~~ won't work as I will be away on holiday from ~~...~~ and when I return every weekend in October and early November has an event which will occupy me fully. ~~...~~ We hold our annual prize giving and Captains weekend and I will be attending at St Andrews an international club manager's conference. After the golf events we shall be closing down ~~...~~ for some months for major ~~...~~ a new irrigation ~~...~~

I hope things take a turn for the better for you.

Yours aye

MENTAL
productions

Queens Gate, School Road, Cirencester
Gloucestershire, GLX 6DU

10th of January 2007

Bismillah Jim,

Yo, Jim, remember me? The stressed television executive from last summer who wrote to you about some TV offers and ended up using you as some kind of weird Scotch confessional? Well, a lot of water has gone under my bridge but I'm now back at work dry as a bone. I say back because, shortly after our last exchange, I was forcibly sectioned under the terms of 1983 Mental Health Act. Some of my more jealous colleagues here at Mental Productions, presumably enraged by my rapid ascent to Executive Development Producer, took action and had me declared insane. I was forcibly shipped off to the famous Priory Rehabilitation Centre. It was a very tough time for me Jim, but, like all things sent to try us, it was a blessing in disguise.

I'm sure you're aware that the Priory is where a lot of Celebrities go to be treated for "laryngitis" and "exhaustion?" That's just PR code for "gone loop the loopy." Basically, Jim, I found myself the only sane man in Crazyville and this did have its advantages. I met a veritable stellar collection of people whilst in there. One of them just happened to be the troubled "singer" Pete Doherty. He had recently gone off on some mad, crazed recording session in the Atlas Mountains of Morocco with some Berbers. While he was there he had picked up little bits and pieces about the world of Islam. One night he sang me a song called "Is Islam Or Isn't It?" It was beautiful and I was transfixed. Through the drunken ramblings of a stoned man/boy genius I came to the biggest decision of my life. I converted to Islam. Such is his will.

Jim, I have never been happier. I now have a new, Islamic name (like Cassius Clay shedding his slave name to be known as Muhammed Ali). My name is now Sheikh Alu Gobi. Do not be afraid when you receive a letter from such a person, it's still me, Dave.

Anyway, there's the background and I'm finally back at work here at Mental Productions. Sadly, I have been demoted to Vice-President In Charge Of Development Duties but it won't be long until I'm back at the top. That's why I'm writing to you again.

Do you remember just before I was declared insane that I made a last minute suggestion about your ~~░░░░░░░░░░░░░░░~~ (peace be upon her) going a couple of rounds with Bruce Lee and his Numchukkas? I know that you were unable to deliver your course as a venue for "Could Bruce Lee Have Beaten Tiger Woods At Golf?" but my last letter got me thinking (TV is fluid Jim, like a river, sometimes flowing fast and strong, sometimes stuck in a stagnant pool to the side of the current, but always fluid).

What would you say to a pro/celebrity golf tournament hosted at your club with the emphasis being a bit more on the side of pro? I can get any ex member of Hear'Say apart from Myleene Klass (peace be upon her) who seems to have been given a second wind by appearing in her bikini on national television. Sadly, such is the culture in which you and I exist.

I think that I can also get Bubble from Big Brother 2 and Bez from the now Unhappy Mondays. Obviously Richard Bacon's up for anything so if you could get the ~~░░░░░~~(Peace be upon her) to play for the celebrity team and provide some pros I think that I could get Bravo to stump up for a pilot.

What do your think my Scotch brother? Do you want to help me get back to the top and claim my rightful position as Executive Development Producer? Do you want to prove to the world that Black Muslim and Scotch can work together in perfect harmony? Do you want to have a crack at getting a coveted TV Quick Award? Of course you do. Let's do some business my tartan comrade and remember-

"If you are the first, then you are a parasite; if the second, then you are an oasis in a desert."- Khalil Gibran

Just one more thing: you: always signed off your letters "yours sincerely" until your epistle of the fifteenth of September which you signed off with "yours aye." What does that mean? I'm guessing that this was a slight softening of your attitude towards me? Maybe some tiny nod to my delicate mental state? Whatever, I appreciate this very human response to a very desperate cry for help. I just thank the prophets (peace be upon them) that I found peace and tranquillity in the very same place as Cat Stevens.

Salaam Aleikum (aye),

داود سلام (DAVE)

Sheikh Alu Gobi
Vice President In Charge Of Development Affairs

MENTAL
productions

Queens Gate, School Road, Cirencester
Gloucestershire, GLX 6DU

7th of Jan 2007

Dear Jim,

Why no speak? Is it because I'm now a Muslim? I hope not? I read this in the madrassah last week- "To you your religion and to me my religion." That is truly how I feel Jim.

If, however your silence is because of what they say on the Kuffar television about us then do not believe any of it. They are media infidels who will receive eternal damnation. You, however, are truly among the chosen and will receive blessed walks with virgins in flowery valleys. But I digress.

Great news! I won my unfair dismissal tribunal on the grounds of racial discrimination and I am now back in my rightful position of Executive Producer. So, just so I cannot be accused of slacking- any news on my proposal?

I am up in ~~xxxxxxx~~ on other business next week and wondered whether I could quickly pop in and sort stuff out face-to-face rather than bothering you with all these letters? I feel it would be far more expeditious. Sadly though, I would now have to pass on the whisky we once discussed..

"Wild is the wind"

Dave

Sheikh Alu Gobi (Dave)

NO REPLY

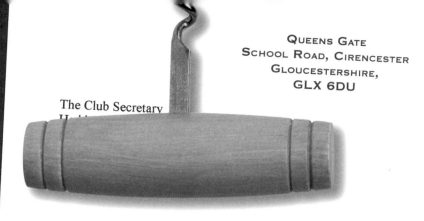

QUEENS GATE
SCHOOL ROAD, CIRENCESTER
GLOUCESTERSHIRE,
GLX 6DU

The Club Secretary

15th Jan 2007

Dear Sir,

I've played many a course in many a country but can honestly say that I've never had a more unpleasant experience than last Thursday's. I was playing your course with my wife, Julia, who is a person of restricted growth accompanying me as my caddy. Maybe we've lead a somewhat sheltered life but throughout our marriage we have never really suffered from any obvious discrimination... until now.

We were just teeing off at the third when I became aware of a couple, of what I took to be ground staff, giggling amongst themselves whilst looking at my wife. One of them said, audibly enough for us to hear, "Why don't you stand up and play?" the other one, obviously emboldened by his brave friend shouted "what's your handicap, your short game?" I know that this might be amusing banter in a public house but this greatly embarrassed my wife and was highly inappropriate behaviour. If it had ended there I might have let it go but, sadly like bullies in the school playground, the whole episode started to snowball.

On the fourth green I noticed the same grounds men talking to a two-ball. They all started laughing and pointing at my wife again, this time one of the golfers pitched in loudly with "careful the bunkers are really deep round here" and the other one laughed and said "it's supposed to get windy later, better tie her down." I remonstrated with the group and asked them whether they were members or staff at the club? They laughed in my face and one of the golfers called me a "midget molester" whilst the other one went down on his knees and simulated a series of sex acts only possible for a person of restricted growth. By now my wife was in tears but on they ploughed. One of the first two then suggested that they "do a bit of dwarf-tossing." We left immediately without talking to anyone at your club.

Looking back at this incident in the cold light of day has made me very, very angry. I demand to know if this sort of behaviour is a regular occurrence at your club? Maybe you feel that somehow golf is for people of "normal" height (in which case you would be wrong, Ronnie Corbett, amusing as he is, is hardly the Jolly Green Giant is he)?
I demand an apology and some form of assurance that this type of behaviour is not condoned by your committee.

Yours truly

Colonel Arthur.J. Lindsay-Bird

Colonel A J Lindsay-Bird
Queens Gate
School Road
Cirencester
Gloucestershire
GLX 6DU

17 January 2007

Dear Colonel Lindsay-Bird,

Thank you for bringing to my attention your recent most unacceptable experience whilst playing here. I read with horror the details of what must have been the most appalling experience for you and your wife especially considering the reasonable distance you had travelled to visit us. Please accept me sincere apologies. In the 8 years I have worked here I have never heard of such an awful incident before. We are regarded by our members and many visitors as a very friendly club with a welcoming attitude.

Clearly this needs immediate and thorough investigation to bring to account those responsible. In order to do this please can you provide me with a little more information so I can follow up and trace those staff and players responsible.

It would be very helpful to know what time you teed off last Thursday (I assume you mean the 11th January). I have looked at our booking sheet and cannot see your name down. Please can you confirm what time you checked in with the pro shop and paid your green fee. Any more information to describe those individuals involved would be helpful too. Fortunately we were very quiet last Thursday so tracing the golfers shouldn't be too difficult.

I once again offer my sincere apologies to you and your wife and please be assured that I will give this my utmost attention to bring those responsible to account. Feel free to write to or telephone me at the club if you prefer (I will be out of the office tomorrow Thurs 18th Jan).

Yours Sincerely,

QUEENS GATE
SCHOOL ROAD, CIRENCESTER
GLOUCESTERSHIRE,
GLX 6DU

18th Jan 2007

Dear Sir,

Thank you for your prompt reply to my letter of the 15th of January regarding the verbal abuse my height-challenged spouse received when we played at your club. I accept your apology. The actions of the great unwashed can hardly be considered your personal fault. If you ask me, the rot set in when they gave them the vote, but I digress.

I was slightly puzzled by your view that the abuse was more upsetting for us because we had travelled a "reasonable distance" to visit you. I'm not entirely sure what you're insinuating? That it would have somehow been less upsetting for Julia if we happened to be residents of the area? I would suggest that, to the contrary, it might have been even more upsetting. It would have dawned on us that the perpetrators of this abuse were locals and that we might expect to get such treatment in the local supermarket, at the doctors, maybe even in church? This kind of thing would never happen in our area as the perpetrator would rapidly find himself smothered in badger fat and nailed to a burning cross in the middle of Golding Woods. We don't muck about round here.

Re your enquiries- I'm afraid that I have a very curious memory in that I can remember certain things in great detail and others, often very recent, are total blanks. I served in Aden and received severe wounds at the Wadi Kbir Uprising. I've killed men in the heat of battle and this tends to do things to the mind. I hope you understand.

I can certainly describe one of the two-ball. He was wearing white golf shoes, brown trousers and a yellow v-neck jumper. He was about six foot, of French appearance and walked with a slight limp on the left hand side. Unfortunately I cannot now recall the other fellow nor can I give a detailed description of the first pair save that they strongly resembled London Cabbies. My friend Colin says that he booked the round for us and he adds that, when I spoke to him about the incident, I mentioned that one of the fellows might have been some sort of children's entertainer/clown from his attire. Does this help?

Yours truly

Colonel Arthur.J. Lindsay-Bird

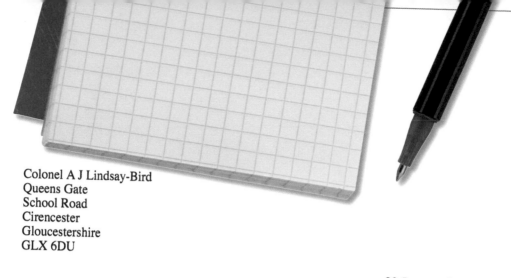

Colonel A J Lindsay-Bird
Queens Gate
School Road
Cirencester
Gloucestershire
GLX 6DU

23 January 2007

Dear Colonel Lindsay-Bird,

Thank you for your reply to my letter regarding the incidents of Thursday 11th January that you have brought to my attention.

Unfortunately I have not yet been able to identify any of those individuals involved so far.

Due to the serious nature of your account of those incidents, I am referring the matter to the local police for further investigation.

Yours Sincerely,

S   tary

26th January 2007

Dear

Thank you for your letter of the 23rd of January replying to my letter of the 18th of the same month.

I am greatly saddened that you have been unable to apprehend any of the "height abusers" despite my best efforts to describe them. My friend Martin who lives in the village was recently sent to a hypnotist by his wife Siobahn (dreadful, bossy woman) to try and put the kybosh on the last remaining pleasure in his life- smoking.

Martin didn't think it would have any effect as he doesn't believe in this sort of mumbo-jumbo. Unfortunately, although he still smokes like a chimney, he now believes that he was Rudolf Hess, the Nazi, in his past life. Although clearly problematic for him, it got me thinking. The point I'm making, in a roundabout way is that I believe that, if Julia and I "go under" we might be able to remember the people involved in the incident with greater clarity.

We are booked into see a certain "Dr" Ballantyne next Thursday. I shall inform you of the results and, hopefully, once we are clearer, you and the local police can track down these miscreants?

Sorry to be a tad unclear but my dog Algeron was buried today. We gave him a Viking funeral in the river Coln (He was Danish) that didn't go entirely to plan. I will be in touch again shortly.

Yours truly

Colonel Arthur.J.Lindsay-Bird

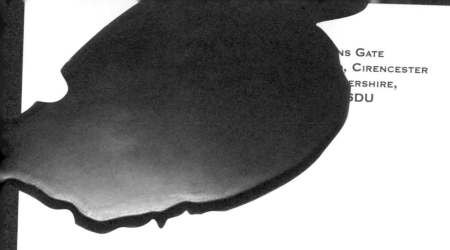

NS GATE

, CIRENCESTER

ERSHIRE,

5DU

Dear Sir,   7th Feb 2007

I told you in my last letter of the 26th of January that Julia and I were going to see a certain Dr
Ballantyne and that I would report back to you. I am a man of my word and there's plenty to tell.

I let Julia go "under" first, as I have to admit that the good doctor looked to be a bit of a "quack"
as we used to call them in the army. I sat to the side of the room as he put her into some form of
trance and started asking questions. It was all very peculiar. Julia adopted a completely different
tone of speech and started to describe scenes of a fairly adult nature from some nineteenth century
"community" of artists that she claimed to have once lived with. I demanded that the doctor bring
her out of her trance immediately. She professed to remembering nothing of the experience but
there was a curious look in her eyes.....

I would have left immediately but we had paid in advance (I know, I know) and so I found myself
lying on the couch looking into the "doctor's" slightly unhinged eyes. That's all I remember. Julia
informs me that I went on in some detail about "Leni Riefenstahl" and the "twinkling lights of
a thousand fires burning as one again." I have absolutely no idea what this was all about and am
only telling you what happened. Julia had the doctor bring me out of my trance when I, apparently,
started speaking German and foaming at the mouth. All very strange and, I'm afraid very
inconclusive.

I'm sorry that this was not of any real help to you regarding your enquiries but I promised to let you
know what happened and I'm a bit of a stickler for principles. If you have any suggestions as to how
either of us can proceed from here I would love to hear from you.

In the meantime, sir, I bid you fair golfing.

Yours truly

Colonel Arthur.J. Lindsay-Bird   NO REPLY

15th Jan 2007

Dear Sir or Madam,

I recently had the opportunity of visiting my old comrade in arms, Colin. We had a very pleasant lunch and a bit of a wander down memory lane to our days in the military. We are both now sadly on "civvy street," have been for quite a few years and have both found it hard to re-adjust to so-called "normal" life. There are times when one wonders just for what reason were we ordered to maim and mutilate in foreign lands? The so-called "uncivilized" foreign enemy now seem, in many respects, far more decent types than the sort of tattooed yobbo that roam the centre of our market towns every evening. But I digress.

Driving back from lunch with my friend I happened to pass by your golf course and, since my clubs, as always, were in the boot, I couldn't help but pop in for a quick round. Golf has always been my escape valve, my little oasis of calm in a terrible world whose horrors I have probably witnessed more than my fair share of. I know that I have killed men in action and that is a terrible cross to bear but let me get to the point-

May I ask, without wishing to be impertinent, whether it is considered normal behavior at your club for another golfer, a complete stranger to myself, someone who looked like a security man at a nightclub or a London taxi driver, to bare his naked backside at me and make obscene gibbon-like noises?

As far as I am aware I did nothing to provoke this incident. Nevertheless the "gentleman" concerned, who assured me in his foul vernacular that he had been a member of your club for some time, followed me for a good three hundred yards shouting "Do you want some, well do you?" whilst scratching and waggling his bare backside in my direction.

I have had something of an anger management problem in the past so I immediately stopped playing and drove home without mentioning the incident to anyone in authority at your establishment. However, in the cold light of day, this incident has considerably perturbed me and I am of a mind to take the matter to the proper authorities unless I receive some form of explanation or apology forthwith.

Yours sincerely,

Colonel Arthur.J.Lindsay-Bird (ret)

The Firs Golf Club, Wellington Road, Upper Merkin
Oxfordshire, OX__ 7W_

Col. A.J. Lindsay-Bird
Queens Gate
School Road
Cirencester
Gloucestershire
GLX 6DU

17/1/07

Dear Colonel Lindsay-Bird

Thank you for your letter of 15th January about your recent visit to ██████ Golf Club.

I am deeply disturbed by the contents of this letter, but before commenting , I would ask you to be kind enough to advise me of the date and exact time of the incident you describe.

25th Jan 2007

Dear Mr ▮▮▮▮▮▮

Thank you for your swift response to my letter of the fifteenth of January. I'm sorry that I haven't been equal to your response time but my dog Algeron passed away last week and I've been most out of sorts ever since. He was a quite remarkable hound- a constant companion to me for the last fifteen years and will be sorely missed. I once inadvertently left him behind after a particularly fine evening at the opera in Buxton, Lancashire. He somehow made it home all the way back down to us here in Gloucestershire, Lord knows how. He was quite the celebrity for a couple of weeks, even making onto "Points West." But I digress.

I'm afraid that I'm very bad with dates. I'm good with faces, bad with dates. I have contacted my friend Colin, whom I was lunching with on the day in question. As this incident happened shortly before Christmas last year, he no longer has his desk diary for that period and is therefore unable to be any more precise than myself. We are both of a certain age I'm afraid. If pushed I would guess that it was somewhere around the twentieth of December, sometime around three o'clock in the afternoon.

I would ask you to keep the details of my dalliance with Roberto completely confidential. It's not that I'm ashamed by all of this. After all, we were close for many years. It's just that I come from a generation that kept these sort of things behind closed doors. I do so hope that you'll understand.

I would be most grateful if you could now "comment" on the incident that I described in my letter of the fifteenth of January. You were not the only fellow to be "disturbed" by it all.

Yours sincerely,

Colonel Arthur.J.Lindsay-Bird (ret)

The Firs Golf Club, Wellington Road, Upper Merkin
Oxf

Colonel A J Lindsay-Bird
Queens Gate
School Road
Cirencester
Gloucestershire
GLX 6DU

29/1/07

Dear Colonel Lindsay-Bird

Thank you for your letter of 25th January.

Having checked our visitors book for the period immediately before Christmas of last year, we can find no record of your having played a████████ all visitors are required to sign in). Furthermore due to the excessively wet weather the course was closed on occasions immediately prior to Christmas.

I am therefore inclined to think that you may have been mistaken about the course you were playing.

As we have no evidence of your having been here or corroboration of the alleged incident we must regard this matter as closed.

30th Jan 2007

Dear Mr ████████

Forgive me for bombarding you with letters. I am aware that you are probably still investigating the bare-bottomed "gibbon" incident but I have a rather embarrassing issue that I need to address.

In my last letter of the 25th of January, a paragraph from another personal letter was somehow included in the letter I sent you. I don't wish to go into too much detail but the paragraph in question deals with my relationship with the Italian defence attaché at the time of my posting in Aden. There is an impending biography that is being written about my life and I am keen to keep as much control over it as possible. The author claims to have certain photographs that I might not want to see the light of day, all poppycock of course, but there are areas of my past that I wish to remain "off-limits" and I would be most grateful if you would keep said details to yourself.

I am just learning to use a microcomputer and have borrowed my son, David's machine. He is in the media and far more computer-literate than myself (aren't they all, they don't know which side their bread is buttered). I'm sorry to have bothered you with this additional matter and hope to hear from you soon in regard to the other matter.

By the by, Algeron was re-buried today. He was from Denmark and we attempted to organise a Viking funeral on the River Coln. The whole village turned out but it was a bit of a washout as the longboat wouldn't stay alight and he drifted down into Fairford which caused quite a fuss. We opted for a more traditional ceremony this time and he is buried beneath his favourite tree in Goldings Woods. God bless his furry soul.

Yours Sincerely,

Colonel Arthur.J.Lindsay-Bird (ret)

NO REPLY

NCESTER
RSHIRE,
X 6DU

13th March 2007

Dear Danish Golfing Friend,

Forgive me for writing to you out of the blue. I know no Danish people apart from a curious fellow who lived in the next village for a couple of years until he exposed himself in church on Harvest Sunday and was asked to leave our community. He was clearly not the sort of person to whom I'd direct my Danish related queries. I'm a very keen golfer so I thought that our mutual love of the game might allow me to seek some advice from you.

Until recently I was the proud and loving owner of Algeron, my Old Danish Chicken Dog (Gammel Dansk Hønsehund). Sadly, he died last Tuesday and is much missed in our home. As Algeron was Danish, we thought it would be fitting to arrange a Viking funeral for him. With the whole village in attendance I carefully placed his furry little body onto a makeshift longboat that I'd made using a drawing from one of my son David's old Ladybird books. I poured some petrol on him and set light to the whole thing. For a moment everything was top-hole and Algeron seemed to be off to Canine Valhalla. But then the fire went out and the remains of his charred body floated off down the river and into the next town where they caused some considerable upset to a biology field trip from the local primary school.

I know you fellows all bury each other in this manner. What is it that I did wrong? Was petrol the right choice petrol or do you use some other form of combustible? I was wondering whether it might have been better to have soaked the body in it overnight? I'm afraid I'm a complete novice at this type of thing and hope that you can help me?

I look forward to hearing back from you. Who knows? If the court case goes my way then I might even make a little trip out to Denmark and play a round on your course?

Yours sincerely,

Colonel Arthur.J.Lindsay-Bird (ret)

GCH
Golf Club Horsholm

Colonel A J Lindsay-Bird
Queens Gate
School Road
Cirencester
Gloucestershire
GLX 6DU

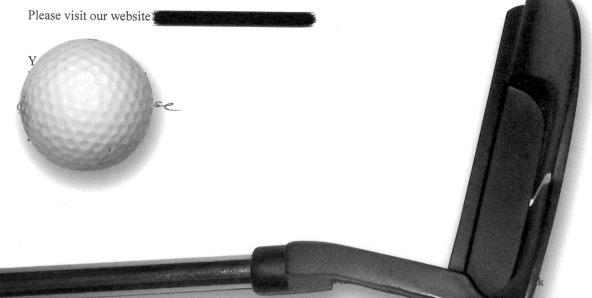

18th April 2007

Dear Colonel Lindsay-Bird,

We have received your letter telling us the sad story about your dog, Algeron's , funeral. I am sure he is sorely missed.

Actually, "we fellows" do not bury each other in the manner you described. Our pets are buried NOT burned.

If you want to try to burn any other item in the future, I would suggest that you make a base of sticks, newspapers and other combustible things, then put the chosen item on top and set it alight from underneath.

For your information I am enclosing the history of ▮▮▮▮▮▮▮ The golf course is a 9-hole par 3 course in the hotel grounds. You shall be very welcome here if you make a trip to Denmark.

Please visit our website ▮▮▮▮▮▮▮

Y

20th April 2007

Dear Mrs ▓▓▓▓▓▓▓▓▓▓

Thank you so much for your slightly tardy reply to my Danish queries. I must firstly apologise for presuming that you burn your dead pets. I assumed that your Viking heritage would have continued and that this would be a fitting end to a furry friend's life? I was simply trying to honour Algeron's ancestral roots and meant no offence.

Having said that, I was intrigued by your fire-lighting tips. You suggest the classic base of sticks (or kindling) newspapers and other combustible things. Well, there's the problem...what might these be? As I explained, it was a Viking tribute funeral so Algeron was on a small long boat and the corpse of a much-loved hound is not immediately combustible especially in a light breeze. I had rather hoped to find out what the Vikings utilized when sending one of your forebears to Valhalla. Despite their slightly roughhouse attitudes towards foreign conquest (I refer, of course, to their rape and pillage philosophy) they were clearly a smart bunch. They must have had some solution to getting their fallen comrades to burn like billy-o?

I must go as my son David is just back from a trip to Scotland where he has been filming a programme called "Would Bruce Lee Have Beaten Tiger Woods At Golf." He works in television and is very important and seems to think that this programme is going to win many awards. He has recently converted to Islam and, between you and me, is a little unbalanced at the moment. I think I need a golfing trip to Denmark, it might calm my frayed nerves.

I do so hope that you can find the time to give me a quick answer re what exactly the Vikings used? I have a pet duck called Steven and he will, one day, pass on and I intend to give him a similar send-off (although he is not Danish, I can't place him geographically). Thank you for your attention to this matter.

Yours faithfully,

Colonel Arthur.J.Lindsay-Bird

GCH
Golf Club Horsholm

Colonel A J Lindsay-Bird
Queens Gate
School Road
Cirencester
Gloucestershire
GLX 6DU

████████████ 5th May 2007

Dear Colonel,

I am sorry you thought my reply tardy. I did not understand that you wanted to know about a Viking funeral. However, I have asked several people including my sister, who has studied ethnology. The general answer is that when the Viking chief died, he and all his faithful companions were put on a longboat. The longboat was set alight on shore, then pushed out to sea, where it burned. The slaves and dogs, horses etc. were killed and buried.

Another person I talked to thought that they had soaked clothes or fur in melted lard, then set I alight.

I hope this will be of some help to you when the time comes for your pet duck, Steven.

This week at the hotel, we have been rushed off our feet with lots of guests in the house. We have had a few public holidays, and that is always a chance for people to have parties. We must not complain – it is good for business. Also the weather has been absolutely brilliant for this time of the year, so many people use our golf course.

Yours sincerely,

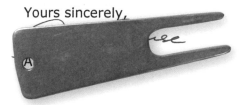

P.S. I see you live in Gloucestershire, we have very good friends there, it is a lovely part of England.

NS GATE
D, CIRENCESTER
TERSHIRE,
6DU

10th May 2007

Dear Mrs ▓▓▓▓▓▓▓▓▓

Thank you so much for your far speedier rely to my letter of the 20th April. Melted lard....who would have thought of it? You Scandinavians certainly are a bright and resourceful bunch. I suppose that's why Ikea took off everywhere although you probably know how to put the blasted flat-packs together? Fortunately, Steven, our pet duck (on whom I've now bestowed honorary Danish citizenship as a mark of respect towards Algeron) is currently in good health so we have no immediate need for another funeral. I do have to admit that I'm keen to try the lard so, if he does pass away...well, every cloud has a silver lining as we say over here.

I'm so glad everything is good for you weather and business-wise. Things over here are not quite so wonderful. My best friend and old colleague-in-arms Colin Muldoon has been thrown out of his golf club for stealing socks from the ladies' locker room laundry basket. It's all very embarrassing and I don't quite know how to broach the subject with him. I know that it's wonderful that you ladies can now play golf but things were a lot simpler in the old days when there was less temptation about.

One last question- you mention at the end of your letter that you have friends here in Gloucestershire. They're not, by chance the Vestergaards? I only say this because my wife, Julia tells me that they are Danish. I don't know them personally or I would have addressed my original enquiries to them. Apparently Harald Vestergaard is quite a character. He lives in a village called Cold Slab and has pretty much taken over the place. Everyone who enters the village pub is forced to wear a horned helmet and he is building a ten-foot statue in the middle of the village in honour of the God Thor. One gentleman objected to this at the parish council meeting and was clove in two with a battle-axe. Everyone knows who did it but they are afraid. If it is the Vestergaards then you must come and see us when you next visit, Harald sounds a right hoot.

Yours sincerely,

Colonel Arthur.J.Lindsay-Bird (ret)

GCH
Golf Club Horsholm

Colonel A J Lindsay-Bird
Queens Gate
School Road
Cirencester
Gloucestershire
GLX 6DU

18th May 2007

Dear Colonel,

Thank you for your letter. We are getting into quite a correspondance! It is fun to hear about all the goings on in your part of the world.

My friends live at ▓▓▓▓▓▓▓▓▓▓▓▓▓ They are (or at least he is) old friends from Cambridge University. They are amongst a group of friends, all from Cambridge-days, who meet up regularly.

My husband and I are off on holiday to ▓▓▓▓▓▓▓ tomorrow, so I have a busy day today.

I am very pleased that Steven has now become an honorary Danish citizen. He is of course not a replacement for Algeron. Have you thought of getting a new dog? Most people who have lost a dog miss it so much. I can understand that Algeron was a very special part of your life.

I am sorry that I don't know the Vestergaards, but he does sound like a right hoot.

Your sincerely,

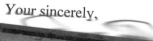

22nd May 2007

Dear Mrs███████████████

Thank you for your last letter. I was also enjoying our correspondence and, to an extent, news of the goings-on within a small Danish Golf course. You have also been most helpful in dealing with my various queries regarding the methods of burial appropriate to animals of Danish origin (naturalized or otherwise).

That said I was horrified to learn in your last letter that you attended "the other place." I am and always will be an Oxford man. I read ornithology at Oriel and gained a gentleman's degree before setting off on my military adventures in the Middle East. I'm afraid that your embarrassing admission leaves me with very little choice but to terminate our relationship. It's nothing personal. I simply can't abide the idea that I should be in some form of regular communication with somebody from that pinko poofter institution.

I have to admit to a tinge of sadness at my decision. It was probably aided by the news in your last letter that you had a husband. I have a wife, Julia but she does not fulfil me in any way. I recently decided to go on a walking holiday in Denmark that Julia accompanied me on. Quite by chance we found ourselves walking all around the ██████ area and I couldn't help but wander in and out of your club on a daily basis. Since Julia accompanied me on the trip I thought it inappropriate to introduce myself officially but know this- you are a handsome woman and if things had turned out differently, I would have made you my wife. Sadly the news that you are married and that you attended such a degenerate academic institution has made this a matter of theory.

I have left you a small token of my esteem buried five yards to the left of the seventh tee in a small tupperware box. I do hope that they will fit and that you will wear them secretly as a sign of respect for our brief friendship. Farewell sweet viking lady.

Yours truly

Colonel Arthur.J.Lindsay-Bird (ret)

GCH
Golf Club Horsholm

Colonel A J Lindsay-Bird
Queens Gate
School Road
Cirencester
Gloucestershire
GLX 6DU

█████████████████ 9th June 2007

Dear Colonel,

My husband and I are back from a lovely holiday. I was very surprised and disappointed to read the contents of your last letter.

I feel I ought to reply in order to put a few facts straight!

I am very sorry that you do not like people from the lovely Cambridge University. I myself attended only the language school for foreigners, while my husband went to ██████ College reading economics and law. Cambridge was where we met.

You said you had been to Denmark and have been in and out of ██████████ Golf club on a daily basis. We DO NOT have a golf club. ██████████ is an hotel and conference center with a small 9-hole golf course attached to it as part of the various sports facilities we offer our guests.

I suspect you have been to ██████████ Golf club, which is close by. People do not just wander in and out of our main building, where the reception is located and I work. I also only work part-time, and I have not seen any couples going in and out on a daily basis. Mostly, people come here for conference or parties. If you really have been here, I find it strange, that you did not introduce yourself.

Just for the hell of it I did go to the 7th tee on our course and found – nothing! I also went to ██████████ club's 7th tee – also nothing! Are you playing a joke on me?

Sincerely,

The Viking Lady

13th June 2007

Dear ██████████

My heart skipped a beat when your letter arrived. I felt so silly for my prejudices and had spent many hours staring at the photographs that I managed to secretly snap of you whilst I was in Denmark. Thank the Lord that you did not attend "the other place." Your attendance at a language school is immaterial. You know as well as I that these institutions serve only to furnish the undergraduates with "foreign oats' in order to alleviate the monotony of their studies. I myself squired a very attractive Tanzanian whilst at Oriel. She could do things I'd only read about in French literature. Of course marriage was out of the question but I still have the memories.....

I most certainly did visit your hotel. I took a taxi from ██████████ (a most peculiar fellow by the name of Torben who wore stockings) to sate my curiosity as to what you looked like. You didn't disappoint. I kept myself incognito as I didn't wish to frighten you. However, I most certainly did leave you a little present under the seventh tee. You might have to do a little digging as I didn't wish to disturb the players but I think it's pretty obvious where it lies.

I'm afraid that I'm not really myself today. My son David, who converted to Islam a while back has been arrested by the police. He was apparently apprehended in an East End "TGI Fridays" wearing what the offciers suspected to be an explosive device. It actually turned out to be some sort of auto-erotic machine but, because he was in robes and on a skateboard..... Prejudice is such a vicious vice. We all have a lot to learn I'm afraid. My other son Randy is a homosexual and I find it very difficult to come to terms with his "interests." I know that you Danish are far more tolerant and you're always having sauna orgies and suchlike. Sadly, we English are so stuck in our ways....maybe if I'd stayed with M'booba M'bendy (the Tanzinian) things would have been different?

I must go now sweet Viking lady. How was Turkey? My grandfather was ripped apart by Turkish scimitars at Gallipoli. He wasn't with the invasion force. He was a botanist and simply strayed into the wrong place at the wrong time having spotted a rare chaffinch. Such, I'm afraid is life. Farewell.

Arthur

Arthur x ♡

NO REPLY

15th January 2007

Sir,

I'm not naïve enough to think that this will get straight to the Tiger himself so a big Happy New Year to whichever minion first deals with this postal communication. My name is Dave Lindsay-Bird and I'm currently in charge of development here at Mental Productions over in the Yookay- your last friend and ally in this increasingly dangerous world.

I know you're busy people so I won't waste your time for too long. Among the myriad of exciting projects that we're developing here at Mental, there's one in particular that I wanted to run by you. It's a television programme called "Could Bruce Lee Have Beaten Tiger Woods At Golf?" The premise is that, since golf is primarily a game of the mind, Bruce Lee would have excelled in the sport. He might even have been able to beat Tiger had he ever picked up a club. Interestingly, his widow, Linda Lee Cadwell, tells us that he had a pathological hatred of the game. He would apparently physically attack any television set that he came across showing the sport- but I digress.

You have to admit it's an interesting thought? We here at Mental specialize in taking take interesting thoughts and turning them into full-blown television extravaganzas. We are currently in final discussions with representatives of ███████████████ to use the beautiful course at ████████ in Scotland as a premium location.

We have already signed up Danny (Shrek) from Hear'Say to play the role of Tiger. We were hoping to use David Yip as Bruce Lee but he has just secured the coveted role of Aladdin in Norwich so we are in negotiations with Ken Hom (the Wok chef) instead.

The basic idea of the show is that we get out two actors to play a round of golf while top scientists (Dr Raj Persaud is on board) and sportsmen (Geoff Capes and Matt Dawson) discuss the strengths and weaknesses of our case.

This is obviously a very exciting project but "where do we come into this?" I hear you cry.

MENTAL productions

Well, I need to organize an hour of "Tiger Time" to interview him for the show. Our presenter, top showbiz personality and devoted golfer, Ross Kemp, will ask him to assess how well Bruce Lee would have done as well as asking Tiger to do some amusing Kung-Fu sounds for the opening title sequence.

We have big, big interest from BBC3Xtra for this project and there's a possibility of a spin-off series with other past and present fictional sporting clashes. Just think of the merchandise/ marketing/advertising potential from these beauties. I'd be prepared to bet my cottage on this idea. I smell TV Quick Awards........

Looking forward to hearing from you my colonial chum,

Dave!

Dave Lindsay-Bird
Senior Executive Development Officer

David Lindsay-Bird
Senior Executive Development Officer
Queens Gate
School Road
Cirencester
Gloucestershire
GLX 6DU

1/ 23/ 2007

Dear Mr Lindsay-Bird,

In short......NO!!

Senior Account Executive

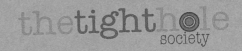

the**tight**h**o**le
society

Queens Gate,
School Road,
Cirencester,
Gloucestershire,
GLX 6DU

The Club Secretary
New Bridge Golf Club
New Bridge
Aberdeenshire
Scotland

2nd Feb 2007

Dear Sir,

I am writing to you regarding a forthcoming event that The Tight Hole Society has planned. We're a friendly gay golf society based in Gloucestershire. We have friends all over the country and we like to try and organise at least four "gay away' days a year.

You'd better lock up your hunky members because, this year, we've decided to pay a little visit to your neck of the woods. Thanks to the new legislation, two of our members, Colin and Alan, got married last year and caravanned all around your area on their honeymoon. I feel like I've already been there as, every hot-tub evening, we are regaled with wild tales of just what a wonderful part of the country it is.

While on their travels they met a very accommodating gentleman by the name of ▬▬▬▬ Jones who highly recommended your club. We were hoping to hold our annual "Randy Admiral Cup" at your establishment sometime in March. Could you let me know what your current availability is?

In total, there would be about eight four-balls and some assorted hangers-on. Ideally, we'd love to use your club facilities for a big gay dinner at the end of the day. If, for any reason this is not possible, then could you recommend a local eatery? Maybe a biker bar or such-like?

I can't wait to meet you all and please do not hesitate to contact me if you have any queeries (geddit??)

Big kisses.

Randy!

Randy Lindsay-Bird
Club Secretary

New Bridge G[...]

07 February 2007

The Tight Hole Society
Queens Gate
School Road
Cirencester
Gloucestershire
GLX 6DU

Dear Sir,

Thank you for your letter dated 2 February 2007.

During March the club is on winter procedures so no pre-booking is needed. Provided the course has not been closed because of snow or frost, just turn up and play. There is an honesty box for your green fees of £12 per player.

The acceptable style of dress at ███████████ is smart/casual. Jackets and ties are not required but <u>the following are not acceptable</u>:
- Denim jeans or track-suits,
- Football/rugby shirts, vests or t-shirts.

Shorts, if worn, should be tailored, not football-style or loose-fitting, and should be worn with socks (long or sports). Shorts are not recommended in March.

The clubhouse will not be open so I suggest that you look at establishments in ████████ (our nearest town) for your dinner.

Yours sincerely,

the tight hole
society

Queens Gate,
School Road,
Cirencester,
Gloucestershire,
GLX 6DU

The Club Secretary
New Bridge Golf Club
New Bridge
Aberdeenshire
Scotland

13th February 2007

Dear (▆▆▆▆▆▆▆

Thank you so much for your letter of the seventh of February in response to mine of the second. The Tight Hole is thrilled and honoured to know that we'll be able to stage our "Randy Admiral Cup" at your club this year. After last year's shenanigans I thought we'd never be allowed to play anywhere again!!

I do have a couple of tiny queries as to your dress code. One of the "Randy Admiral" traditions is that of a different costume theme each year. This year, in honour of our host country, the theme is "Hotpants and Tartan." I note from your letter that shorts should be "tailored, not football style or loose-fitting..." Whilst most leather hotpants are certainly not loose fitting, they are not quite tailored either (although they are certainly a very snug fit!!). Would these be acceptable if we agreed that they would all be of the buttock covering type with a strict ban on the more "airy" versions?

Also, some of our members are going the whole hog and become very "creative" in their designs. Before they embark on their sartorial journeys, is there a particular tartan that they should avoid because some clan murdered another way back? Is there a local tartan that might be preferable? Do you know of any tartan with pink in it? So many questions, I know but I like to get things just right and to not cause too much offence upon arrival. I'll admit to being very ignorant of tartan politics- my only real knowledge is gleaned from the film "Braveheart" starring the dreamy, ▆▆▆▆▆▆▆▆▆ troubled entity that is Mel Gibson.

Finally, (thank the Lord, I hear you cry) I notice that you recommend the town of ▆▆▆▆▆▆ for our post golf Bacchanalia. Do your (or your husband) happen to know if there is much of a "scene" in the town? What about hotels? If we encounter any "attitude" problems we might be forced to stick our tent poles into your soggy turf. Is there somewhere in the grounds of the course where we could camp should everything go wrong?

Big kisses,

Randy!

Randy Lindsay-Bird

NO REPLY

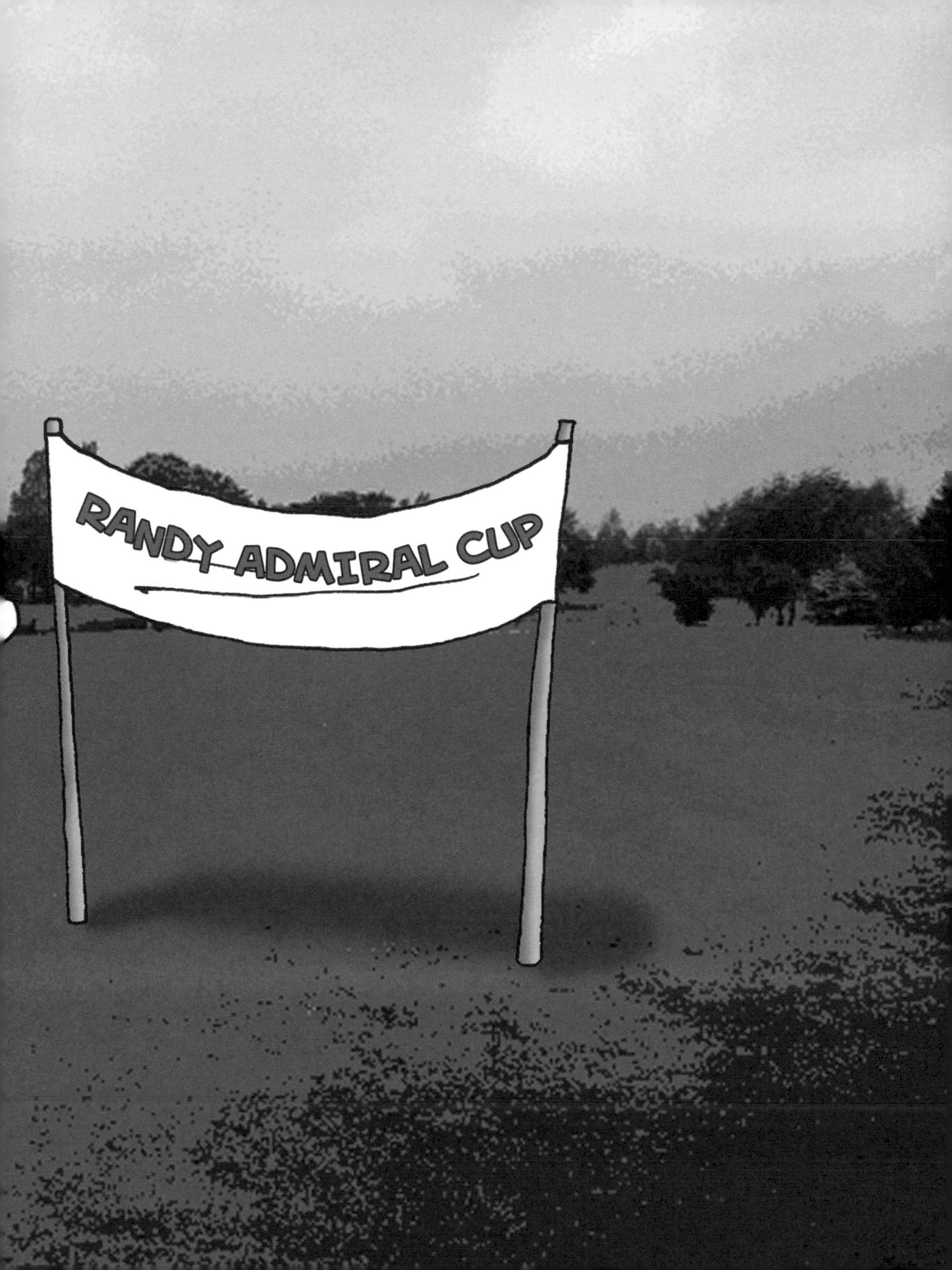
RANDY ADMIRAL CUP

QUEENS GATE
SCHOOL ROAD, CIRENCESTER
GLOUCESTERSHIRE,
GLX 6DU

The Club Secretary

5th March 2007

Dear Sir,

My wife and I were recently over in Ireland to visit my old friend Colin Muldoon at his home in ███████ He and I served together in Aden and he saved my life during the Wadi Kbir Uprising and we try to see each other at least twice a year. Having enjoyed a pleasant weekend we took the opportunity of a little detour on our way home to play a round on your course. This was at Colin's recommendation

All went swimmingly for a while with my wife acting as caddy and myself playing unexpectedly well. Things, however, then took a slightly curious turn. I was disturbed by an odd sound from the direction of the beach. It sounded like someone was in pain. I immediately went over to see what the trouble was.

Lying on the other side of a dune with their backs to the sea were two "gentlemen" who appeared, from the top half of their clothing, to be fishermen. I say top-half because all three were trouser-less and hunched over something that appeared to be a dead skate. Not to put too fine a point on it, one of the pair seemed to be in "flagrante delicto" with said dead sea-creature.

I managed to avoid my wife witnessing this revolting scene and we left your premises immediately. I write simply to inform you of the "goings on" on your beach and to urge you to do something about it. I have long heard the legend of lonely fishermen using the tubular body of a Skate as a so called "fisherman's friend" but hardly expected to have this "myth" made reality on a golf course.

I look forward to hearing from you re action taken.

Yours sincerely,

Colonel Arthur.J.Lindsay-Bird (ret)

North Downs Golf and Country Club
Beltra, Sligo, Ireland

North Downs Men's Golf Club

T. 2292

Date: 11th March 2007

To: Col. Lindsay-Bird,

Dear Sir,

I am in receipt of your astonishing letter of 5/3/07.

If I am to be able to progress further I need top know the date on which your wife and yourself played ~~a match~~

Our next Committee meeting will be at the end of the month so a prompt reply would be appreciated.

Yours Sincerely

The Club Secretary
North Downs Golf and Country Club

Beltra
Sligo   26th March 2007
Ireland

Dear Sir,

Thank you for you reply to my letter regarding the unfortunate "incident" that took place on your golf course. I apologise for the delay in my getting back to you but I have been away in Germany visiting the Wolf's Lair in Rastenburg. As an ex-military man I have a profound fascination for the psychology that lies behind great power. But I digress.

I must say that I was quite surprised by the tone of your letter. Your demanding to know the date upon which my wife and I were at your golf course seems to somehow indicate that there are certain days of the week where the behaviour that I witnessed is somehow acceptable at your establishment.

I have played golf all over the world and have never, ever come across such a scene as the one I saw that day. It remains burned on my memory. I would have hoped that a respectable club would take immediate action to make sure that this kind of perversion would never, ever be allowed to happen again. I would also have expected some form of apology, That, sir, would have been my first instinct but maybe I'm old-fashioned?

My friend Alan keeps a desk diary so it might be better for you to consult him if you continue to require a date for the incident. Quite what this particular information will achieve is beyond me. What I require from you is some form of assurance that this type of behaviour is not condoned by your club, and that you will take all appropriate measures to see that no other golfer is ever subjected to this kind of sordid spectacle.

I await your reply with great anticipation and hope that I will not have to take this matter further.

Yours sincerely,

NO REPLY

Colonel Arthur.J.Lindsay-Bird (ret)

QUEENS GATE
SCHOOL ROAD, CIRENCESTER
GLOUCESTERSHIRE,
GLX 6DU

The Club Secretary
Dale Golf Club Ltd
Harry Hill
Broadstone
Oxfordshire
OX29 6TF

5th March 2007

Dear Sir (I presume it's a Sir)

I was hoping that you might be able to help me in a slightly delicate matter. I'll cut to the chase; I'm a woman of a certain age whose husband is…..well, let's just say, in the words of the song: "the thrill is gone."

I suspect that he is "playing away from home" but have no actual proof of this- until yesterday. He recently went away on "business" and spent a couple of nights away from our marital home. He claimed that he'd been in London attending a conference but, when he returned, I searched his pockets and found a receipt from your club in his sports jacket.

I am not aware that he even plays golf but, if he did, he'd have no reason to hide it from me. I would be more than happy to get the lazy bastard out of the house occasionally. All he does is sit in front of the television scratching his testicles while salivating over that Jezebel, Claudia Winkelman on "Strictly Come Dancing Extra."

Could you let me know whether he was playing golf at your course last week and, if so, who with? Do you have overnight rooms at your establishment? Are women allowed on your premises? Forgive me for my enquiries but I need to know as much as possible before I confront him. I'd actually be rather thrilled if he was "playing away" as I could then file for divorce, get as much of the little cash that he has and try to start again before I hit the bargain bin.

My husband's name is Arthur Lindsay-Bird although he sometimes uses the name Colonel Hawk- don't ask me why, it's an army thing. I hope that you can help me in a discreet manner with this enquiry and that I shan't have to pay you a visit to get the information that I require?

Yours truly,

Julia.S.Lindsay-Bird (Mrs)

Mrs Julia Lindsay-Bird
Queens Gate
School Road
Cirencester
Gloucestershire
GLX 6DU

20th March 2007

Dear Mrs Lindsay-Bird,

Upon receipt of your letter dated 5th March I have checked back through our visitor records, it does not appear that your husband has played golf here.

We do not have any accommodation on site.

In our club Women have exactly the same privileges and rights that men do.

Golf Coordinator

QUEENS GATE
SCHOOL ROAD, CIRENCESTER
GLOUCESTERSHIRE,
GLX 6DU

The Club Secretary
Dale Golf Club Ltd
Harry Hill
Broadstone
Oxfordshire
OX29 6TF

30th March 2007

Dear Mr ▓▓▓▓

Thank your for your letter of the 20th March in reply to my letter of the 5th. Forgive me for the delay in writing back to you but I have been in Rastenburg with Arthur visiting the Wolf's Lair. He has an unhealthy obsession with the Second World War that I do not share. You're a man. I presume you simply love the idea of wandering around some creepy Prussian woods taking photographs of ruined concrete bunkers in which Hitler once did his nasty business? Call me old-fashioned, but I'm more of a Hotel Du Cap kind of girl. I once stayed there for a weekend with the drummer from Procul Harum, but I digress.

I am thrilled to hear that you have no record of Arthur playing golf at your establishment and that you do not have accommodation on site. However, this still leaves me with the problem of an unexplained bar receipt from your club. Why would a man who rarely leaves the safety of his living room chair travel all the way to wherever ▓▓▓▓ is for a drink at your bar? You clearly state that women are allowed in your bar. It is therefore, not beyond the bounds of reason that Arthur went there to meet one? Am I wrong?

Clearly he wasn't using his real name. Would it be possible for you to just ask some of the regulars at your bar whether anyone using the name "Colonel Hawk" had been in?
If so, who was he with? He has an eye-patch and a pronounced limp from his involvement in the violent suppression of the Wadi Kbir uprising in Aden.

I've been through enough Mr ▓▓▓▓ believe me. Arthur took over the family business from my father and drank it into the ground. He went bankrupt and then started this ludicrous Iraqi "security" company that has made him think he's back in the SAS again.

I can't afford to leave him unless you supply me with the proof. I rely on your sense of decency and fairness. I'm sure you don't want your club used as some kind of adulterous meeting place any more than I do?

Yours truly,

Julia B

Julia.S.Lindsay-Bird (Mrs)

Mrs Julia Lindsay-Bird
Queens Gate
School Road
Cirencester
Gloucestershire
GLX 6DU

8th May 2007

Dear Mrs. Lindsay-Bird,

Upon receiving your second letter with regards to the whereabouts of your husband "Colonel Hawk", I regret to inform you that none of our regulars have seen your husband.

I have also asked ouor bar manager Mr. ████████ if he has seen your husband at the club, however I again regret to infom you of his negative reply.
He also stated that he would have definetly remembered a customer with such unique physical characteristics as your husband of indeed such a memorable name as "Colonel Hawk".

Please find enclosed a copy of our bar receipt as you can see it does not show the golf clubs details, and we are therefore unsure of how you can determine the bar receipt found in your husband's jacket is from the ████████ Golf Club.

Sorry I could not assist you in your investigation any further and good luck in the future.

Golf Coordinator/PGA Professional.

NO REPLY

QUEENS GATE
SCHOOL ROAD, CIRENCESTER
GLOUCESTERSHIRE,
GLX 6DU

The Club Secretary

 Golf Club,

13th April 2007

Sir,

I was a recent guest at your establishment at the invitation of one of your members, whose name I would prefer to keep private as he does not wish to be involved. I'm not a golfer, although I'm married to one for my sins. The Colonel has spent more time on fairways than he's had hot dinners so I'm an experienced golf widow. I'm telling you this not for sympathy but to impress on you that I'm not some sort of hysterical woman who doesn't understand the normal ways of the golf world.

So, about three weeks ago, I was at your place for lunch and all was going swimmingly. I was enjoying a good lunch and a chinwag with my companions. It was then that some movement outside caught my attention. To my astonishment, a "gentleman" in a dirty polar bear costume was simulating a lewd sex act with another "gentleman" in full golf garb. These perverted activities went on for about three minutes right in front of us as though they were in the privacy of their own homes.

It took place in full view of the window that I was sitting next to. My other two companions also witnessed this event and were equally appalled. When the "show" was over, we found that we had all lost our appetite and left immediately. In hindsight, we should have complained to someone at the club but one of our party was really in some distress and wanted to go home immediately.

I write firstly to inform you of the goings-on at your club and to demand an apology. I am not a "stick in the mud" and have a sense of humour but this was beyond the pale. Maybe your club has a certain attitude or standards that are different from golf clubs that I am used to? If this is the case then visitors should at least be warned upon arrival.

I thank you for your urgent attention to this matter.

Yours etc,

Julia Lindsay-Bird (Mrs)

Oak Woods Country Club

Rottingham, Bristol. BS3 7RX

Mrs Julia Lindsay-Bird
Queens Gate
School Road
Cirencester
Gloucestershire
GLX 6DU

18 April 2007.

Dear Madam

Polar Bear Incident.

What a dreadful shock for you to have to deal with especially after everything was going so perfectly on your day with us.

As you can see from the attached poster we are right on the culprits trail and other first time guests here hopefully will be spared the obvious embarrassment.

To make amends why not give us another chance and come back for another lunch. The chef has promised not to include the magic mushrooms in the omelette. You could even suggest to The Colonel that he lends you his shot gun in case the old blighter pops up again. A backside full of lead would no doubt put an end to our friends amorous advances and save me the trouble of having to write letters like this to traumatised ladies.

Warmest regards

IMPORTANT SAFETY NOTICE

Following the reported sighting of a potentially dangerous and obscene polar bear (CCTV image below) on the course we would like to warn all visitors to be on their guard.

We have taken advice from Bristol Zoo on this matter, and have the following advice should you happen to encounter this beast on the premises:

1. **Don't run -** *the bear may see you as prey or a potential mate, and chase you.*
2. **Don't give it food or drink -** *the bear will probably be hungry being this far away from it's natural territory, so your bar bill is likely to be quite high.*
3. **Calmly and quietly find a member of staff -** *the Zoo has loaned us a number of tranquiliser guns in order to capture the beast.*

Thank you for your assistance.

QUEENS GATE
SCHOOL ROAD, CIRENCESTER
GLOUCESTERSHIRE,
GLX 6DU

Heath And Safety Officer

10th May 2007

Dear Mr

Thank you for your letter of the 18th of April in reply to mine of the 13th. I'm sorry that it's taken me this long to reply but I have been away with my husband on a walking holiday in Northern Denmark. It was a very tiring two weeks and I can barely stand up let alone write a letter at the moment. The Colonel has made friends with a lady from a golf club out there. It's quite a spectacular place and if you ever pay a visit to the country you should try and visit. They are exceptionally polite...unlike yourself.

Forgive me, but re-reading your letter, I get the feeling that you didn't take my complaint entirely seriously? I know that it must have been an unusual thing to deal with but that doesn't make it any more acceptable. Believe me, I would be more than happy to turn up with the Colonel's twelve-bore and give the lot of you "backsides full of lead." I presume that you come from the school of thought that believes that there is no place for women on a golf course? Let me tell you something, if it wasn't for women like me cooking your suppers, washing your dirty underwear and generally keeping your sad, pathetic, whisky-soaked lives on the road, you'd all be sleeping in cardboard boxes under a bridge.

I've spent thirty odd years putting up with your sort- fat, blazer-wearing cads who can't handle anything but another jug of port. I'm glad that you find people simulating homosexual activity on your course to be amusing. Maybe it's some ritual initiation that new "members' are required to go through before they can join your establishment? Whatever the case, I shan't be returning and neither will any of my companions. I presume you don't care? I am sending a copy of our correspondence to the Herald Courier. They have already expressed great interest in this story. I shall also be showing this correspondence to the Colonel. I feel confident that, should I not receive an acceptable apology, you will be receiving a visit from him in person.

Yours truly

Julia Lindsay-Bird (Mrs)

NO REPLY

MENTAL
productions

Queens Gate, School Road, Cirencester
Gloucestershire, GLX 6DU

The Club Secretary
Sandy Bay Country Club
Sandy Bay
Inverness
AD5 4TY

Yo,

10th May 2007

I'm Dave Lindsay-Bird and I pretty much run the ideas department here at Mental Productions. We're a funky-monkey, kick-ass production company that's making waves in the sea of show-biz-ness right now. Just last week we cleaned up at the TV Quick Awards with honours all round for "Golf On Drugs" with Snoop Doggy Dog and the coveted "TV Quick Infotainment Show Of The Year" for "Could Bruce Lee Have Beaten Tiger Woods At Golf?" Without tooting my own horn, I'm doing pretty damn good right now and consequently have quite a lot of bread to blow on my next project.

So why's this important TV guy writing to me at my golf club, I hear you cry? Well, you might have gathered from the two programmes I mentioned above that I'm a golf nut and that golf is HOT (sizzlewizzle) right now on the goggle box. I have an idea that I want to run by you that would be filmed on your golf course (Lamarr, the pop star told me about your place).

Here's the idea- it's called "Golf War 3" (Geddit??? Gulf war etc). The idea is a cracker. Two celebrity four-balls tee off for eighteen holes of golf. So far, so boring right??? Wrong!!!

The twist, TV always has a twist, it's the LAW!! The twist is that there are landmines (not real ones relax!!) buried along the course that explode and cover the celebrities in purple dye. There are also paint-ball snipers hidden in the heather and a clown who drives around in a golf cart trying to run the celebrities over. If either team manages to complete the round without being blown up, shot or run-over by the clown then they win. Simple eh!!!

ITV have gone nuts about the idea and we have already got Jamie Theakston and Piers Morgan to captain the two teams. We would need the use of your course for two days sometime in May for which we could pay £150,000. What do you think? Write back quick and let's talk turkey.

Peace, out,

Dave!

Dave Lindsay-Bird
Executive Vice-President

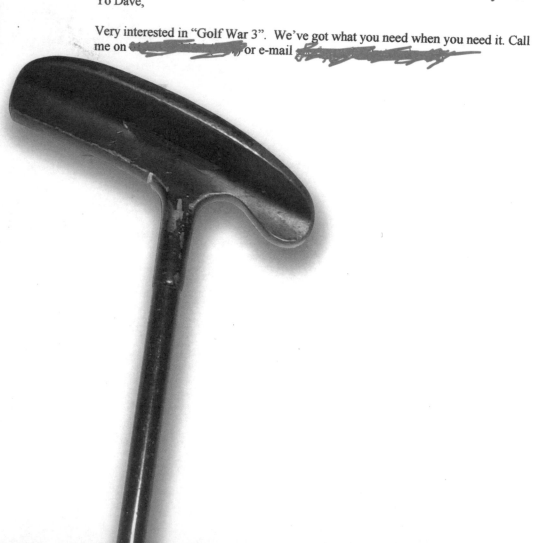

Sandy Bay
Country Club

Sandy bay
Country Club
Sandy Bay
Inverness
AD5 4TY

Dave Lindsay-Bird
Mental Productions.
Queens Gate
School Road
Cirencester
Gloucestershire
GLX 6DU

14th May 2007

Yo Dave,

Very interested in "Golf War 3". We've got what you need when you need it. Call me on ~~████████~~ or e-mail ~~████████~~

productions

Queens Gate, School Road, Cirencester
Gloucestershire, GLX 6DU

The Club Secretary
Sandy Bay Country Club
Sandy Bay
Inverness
AD5 4TY

16th May 2007

nuqneH

I can't believe you speak Klingon dude, that's so radical. When I sent my letter to you I was really worried that "golf people" wouldn't get my vision and see how cool "Golf War 3" would be for the game. I assumed that you were all probably racist, misogynistic crusty old bastards who wouldn't give television the time of day. Well how wrong was I!!

Re your letter, we are not currently on-line as we have a stoopid head honcho who is pretty traditional for television and thinks that we'd spend our whole day downloading pornography (he's right!!). I'm therefore forced to write by snail mail as I need a record of our discussions for the lawyers- sorry dude, but it's THE LAW!!

To business- you say you've got what we need, when we need it- excellent. Ideally we are looking to film the pilot in two weeks time!! I know it's tight but the channel want to get this rolling so that we get a possible series on air for Christmas. If this is a green light then we'll need to send up the teccies (not the Trekkies the Teccies) to do a site survey and to start burying the cable network (approx seven miles we think). I also want to send up the armourer so that he can start looking at where the landmines can be placed. The channel is keen for us to have as much whiz-bang as possible so we are now in discussion with a company who claim we can use mortars and some form of revamped cluster bomb that they bought off the Israelis. They're also being a bit weird about the clown. They're not cool on a clown car. I wondered whether we could use one of those caged ball pick-up machines that they use on driving ranges? Do you have one of those? My thought is that we could "Mad Max" it up and put some spikes and stuff on the front that Clownie could use to pierce Piers Morgan's buttocks (very popular everywhere that one).

I can't tell you how excited we are that this is going to happen. Are there hotels near you or will we be put up in quaint little local cottages and live with the local ▆▆▆▆? This would be fine for most of the crew but I'm afraid that I wouldn't be able to do that. I'll need more executive facilities. Please advise ASAP as "time is money" (that's what President Nasser of Egypt used to say all the time) I smell Baftas!!!!

Buy' ngop

Dave!

Dave Lindsay-Bird

Dave Lindsay-Bird
Mental Productions.
Queens Gate
School Road
Cirencester
Gloucestershire
GLX 6DU

Sandy Bay
Country Club
Sandy Bay
Inverness
AD5 4TY

nuqneH Dave

Sadly I don't speak TLHINGON as well as I would like but I use it from time to time because I like their attitude on matters of Qapla' batlh je. Most people miss the point. I am very impressed that you didn't.

qep'a'mey: I can provide accommodation for up to eight people in self-catering steadings (⬛⬛⬛⬛⬛⬛⬛⬛) any time up until the end of May. More "executive facilities" are available locally (within 25mins drive) see below.

Our golf course is ideally set up for rural gorilla warfare but offers the tactically aware golf celebrity the opportunity to play them selves into easily defendable positions (if they can hit the ball straight). All of the holes are lined on at least one side with gorse where cables and, more importantly, snipers could be easily concealed thus saving a lot of digging. We don't have a caged ball collector but could probably get one at short notice. I will look into it.

Have you considered making the celebrities compete head to head on the early holes for tactical defence equipment such as CGI personal shield generators and/or group shield generators? The needs of the many out weighing the needs of few, and all that. This could lead up to the final confrontation on the 18th fairway where a CGI Warbird decloaks and gives it paint bomb proton torpedoes with both barrels to any celebrity who was foolish enough to waist their shields in earlier confrontations. Although this does away with the clown you will now require a helmsman and a weapons officer for the Warbird (the potential for whiz-bang seems limitless). Am I getting OTT?

mupwI' yI'uchtah!

MENTAL
productions

Queens Gate, School Road, Cirencester
Gloucestershire, GLX 6DU

The Club Secretary
Sandy Bay Country Club
Sandy Bay
Inverness
AD5 4TY

19th May 2007

epetai-zana Al,

Thank you for your top speedy response. You're my kind of guy. You should have been in the glamorous world of television instead of some of the low-life bastards that slip and slide through the cesspools of this industry....I'm a bit depressed Al. The fourteen-year old bastard who runs the channel has now suddenly decided that "Golf War 3" is too "yesterday." He has apparently decided to run with another bloody Ross Kemp vehicle in which he plays crazy golf with ex-underworld killers. This is all because Kemp fluked a BAFTA nomination for his "Gangs" series and can walk on water at the moment.

All, however, is not lost. I am currently in emergency discussions with the Bravo Channel who are really quality, much better than ITV, and seem very interested. This, sadly, is the world I inhabit Al. One day it's all systems go and the next...it's head in the gas oven time. I'll come clean brother. I had a shattering nervous breakdown some time back and converted to Islam as a direct result of an intense experience during my recovery period.

"If God brings you to it, He will bring you through it. In happy moments, praise God. In difficult moments, seek God. In quiet moments, worship God. In painful moments, trust God. In every moment, thank God".

I want you to know this Al. I brought you this project and will not let it run away. This is my word. The budget might now be slightly smaller than originally discussed but we can still make a good programme? Time is really of the essence now if we want to make this work. Let me know your minimum location figure for two days. Bravo will want to make the clown more mega-aggressive. I'm cool with that but what kind of insurance does your place have?

I can't even think straight right now Al. I'm really bummed out. I thought the deal was sealed and then they pull it away. I need it to work or the wolves will eat me up here at Mental. I can already see them whispering by the "babyfoot" table sensing a kill. Once again it's "let's kick the black man while he's down time." Write me fast and I can save this. Otherwise I'll be "strange fruit hangin' from the poplar trees." Forgive me for all this Al. I'm counting on you man. Bismillah.

Dave

Dave

Sandy Bay
Country Club

Dave Lindsay-Bird
Mental Productions.
Queens Gate
School Road
Cirencester
Gloucestershire
GLX 6DU

Sandy Bay
Country Club
Sandy Bay
Inverness
AD5 4TY

22nd May 2007

nuqneH Dave

I am humbled by your command of TlhIngan hol (and English) and respect a man who is at peace with his Qun. Don't get stressed because you think you may be letting us down in some way. You seem like one of the good guys and it will please me if we can help you. What's for you won't go past you (Scottish proverb). Be cool.

Our golf course's very existence is under threat from greedy fool developers. The £150K you mentioned at first contact was exactly the amount required to save the place. It seemed like manner from heaven. We all had our fingers crossed but I had cautioned all concerned that if something seems to good to be true it probably is.

I do not understand how finances are agreed in the world you occupy I will therefore need to rely on you to negotiate the best deal that you can on our behalf. The closer you get to £150K the greater chance we have of survival. Do us proud brother.

If you do the deal and war breaks out on our golf course you will not be covered by our insurance (there is a plethora or clauses regarding insurrection) so I'm afraid you will have to make your own arrangements

mu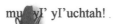yI' yI'uchtah!

productions

Queens Gate, School Road, Cirencester
Gloucestershire, GLX 6DU

The Club Secretary
Sandy Bay Country Club
Sandy Bay
Inverness
AD5 4TY

24th May 2007

nunqeH Al,

Your letter killed me dude. I can't believe that the big corporate wolves are growling at your doorway up wherever it is that you are. What the hell are developers hassling you for? It's not like anyone wants to live there surely?

"Tell me where do the children play?" Yusuf Islam (Cat Stevens)

Things have spiralled into an abyss of despair down here. You probably heard that Ross Kemp won the Bafta? Can you believe it? This means the guy could now get a show of himself farting into a chimps' mouth commissioned if he fancied it. He's got our balls in a vice and he's starting to turn the screws. Two weeks, ago...TWO WEEKS AGO....I was the hottest property in infotainment development and now it's like I've got man flu. By the way Bravo have passed on "Golf War Three" but don't worry, they weren't right for the project anyway.

The exciting news is that I now have a dial-up web-caster interested in the project. This is so much better than prime-time television because it means that technically the whole world can now watch our show...cool huh!! Obviously the budgets are not quite the same league but we can start small and then name our price when we're hot again. They currently have two hundred pounds for a location fee but I'm playing hardball and think we can get it up to two hundred and fifty. Oh...Theakston and Morgan have pulled out as well but we don't need them, they're losers. I've got Bubble from Big Brother Three and Handy Andy (did brilliantly on Sky One's amazing "Cirque De Celebrité) pencilled in.

I'm doing everything I can for you bwana. Last night I stayed up and off the crack just thinking and pacing round my loft. I wanted to work out a way that we could pull this off and stick it to the Man. Then it came to me. Maybe we play on the fact that you've got developers coming in? We make it a bit like "Restoration" (which they've just canned, probably so that they can pay for "Ross Kemp And His Amazing Methane Monkeys"). We get the celebrities to play to save your golf course? Is there some USP that your place has?

Is it the oldest course in Scotland? Did Robert the Bruce play there? Have the Krankies ever visited? Anything you can think of. We can lie about it if you can't think of anything important. Then we'll play the sympathy card to get everyone on board and maybe even get it onto the Beeb, they love ethnic shit.

Put your thinking sporran on Alf and write me back quick as time is money. Give me something I can work with. If it works out then we can get on with blowing the fuck out of your place. Fingers crossed.

"I believe in black man Ray."

Dave !

Dave

NO REPLY

Queens Gate, School Road, Cirencester
Gloucestershire, GLX 6DU

The Club Secretary,
Clearlake Course,
100 Clearlake Street,
Mountview
WA 47832

Sir,   13th May 2007

I'm senior Vice-President here at Mental Productions in the UK and I'm writing to you at the behest of Bonny Langford who said, and I quote: "I love that place, it's brilliant." We've made programmes like- "Too Many Cooks..." where top celebrity chefs Greco-Roman wrestle each other for the opportunity of staying on a desert island with a bevy of beautiful (lady) pastry chefs- this will be airing on Fox this Fall.

I'm writing to you because I also run a talent agency called "Mental Talent." I now represent some of the biggest name currently working in the UK. People on my books already include: Noel from Hear'Say, Craig McLachlan from Neighbors, top models like Jodie Marsh and Hawkwind as well as multi-talents like Keith Chegwin.

Now what in God's name has this got to do with the good game of golf or myself? Good question, here's the answer- I'm launching "Mental American Talent USA" and want to stage a huge PR event to kick-start this new company. I've persuaded Joe Pasquale (a scratch golfer) to host a one-off Celebrity Pro-Am in which all of my UK talent would play in a golf competition with established US entertainers. I can tell you now that Lady Henrietta Hervey (the youngest of the famous troika) has never played golf on TV before so you've got a real royal scoop straight up!

Let's talk turkey! I have $500,000 in play for location fees for which I'd need use of your place for a two-day competition. We have big time sponsorship in the bag and need to get moving on this.

Yours etc,

Dave!

Dave Lindsay-Bird
Senior Vice-President

NO REPLY

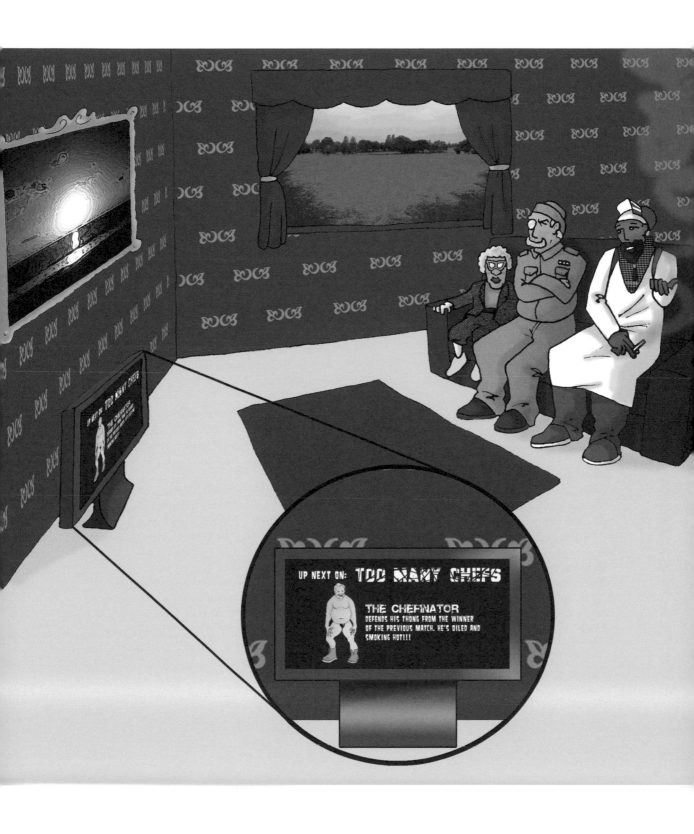

QUEENS GATE
SCHOOL ROAD, CIRENCESTER
GLOUCESTERSHIRE,
GLX 6DU

The Club Secretary
Oak Woods Country Club
Rottingham
Shropshire
ST56 7RX

20th April 2007

Dear Sir,

I was hoping to come and play a round of golf at your course as a friend of mine, Ronnie Mallinson, never stops going on about what a great place it is to play. Before I make the journey, (I work forty minutes away from you) I had a couple of queries.

Do you permit the use of private golf carts? I'm a bit of an amateur inventor and idle away the ever-decreasing amount of spare time that my wife Julia allows me making "custom" carts. My new pride and joy is Arthur 3, a fully automated, elevated buggy that responds to my every golfing need. It's a totally roadworthy vehicle with all the certificates and stuff.

The whole thing started when I first used "normal" golf carts after I came back from Gulf War One. With my left leg badly mutilated I was forced to take to motorised transport. I was immediately dissatisfied with the quality of your average buggy and decided to do something about it. Four years later and Arthur 3 was born. I've appeared with her on Blue Peter, Points West and won the gold medal on "Hooginvetor" (Belgian TV).

A tad of technical stuff, although a quadraped, it does not cause the damage to earth that most people assume. Arthur 3, unlike versions 1 and 2 is lightweight and reasonably agile. It can do 0-60 on any surface in under fifteen seconds so, it's no slouch. Unlike normal buggies you won't find my four-ball taking four hours to play eighteen holes, we can normally be in the 19th on our second G&T in under two hours. This could double the playtime available to you and your members- more importantly it'll also double your money.

As long as you're agreeable I'll bring Arthur 3 along, play a round and then give you an off-road wander if you fancy. You'll be ordering some for your club within minutes. I attach a photo for your perusal.

Arthur 3

Yours sincerely,

Colonel Arthur.J.Lindsay-Bird (ret)

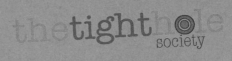
the**tight**h⊙le
society

Queens Gate,
School Road,
Cirencester,
Gloucestershire,
GLX 6DU

The Club Secretary
Stockbridge Golf Club
Fordington
Surrey
FO89 YTB

21st April 2007

Hi!!!

I run ▓▓▓▓▓▓▓▓ friendliest little gay golfing society. We don't exactly have a "home club" but just tend to use different venues for our different events. We're all still high as kites at the success of our "Randy Admiral" Cup that we held at the beautiful ▓▓ as kites at the success of our "Randy Admiral" Cup that we held at the beautiful ▓▓ ▓▓▓▓▓▓" course in ▓▓▓▓▓▓ last month. We had twenty-two members join us in this beautiful setting and we partied like it was 1999 (and played some golf). I presume that you might have read in the press about one particular incident and I do not wish to draw any more attention to the matter save to say that the whole thing was grossly exaggerated and no animal was harmed in any way throughout the entire weekend. We still live, sadly, in an age of some bigotry, especially in some of the right-wing press.

But enough of my waffling, why am I contacting you? You might know my father, Colonel Arthur Lindsay-Bird? He's a keen golfer and has played pretty much every course in ▓▓▓▓▓▓▓▓ and ▓▓▓▓▓▓▓ since he moved back to "The Homeland" after many years in the Middle East? Not to put too fine a point on it, he comes from a generation that was never taught to be totally at ease with homosexuality. I do not blame him for this but it has, sadly, meant that we have always had a somewhat fractious relationship. He's always preferred my brother David, who is, apparently, more of a "family man."

Here's my point (finally!!). My father is approaching his eightieth birthday and I thought it might be the ideal moment to both celebrate his life and show him that us "poofters" as he insists on calling us, are not all the "spawn of Satan." I was wondering how much it would cost to rent out your club for a day on Thursday the 18th of May, the Colonel's birthday? I thought it would be great fun to hold our annual "Pink Pounder" competition and have him as our guest of honour. There'd be forty or so of our members plus about ten of my immediate family. The plan would be to play a round of golf in the afternoon followed by a big gay dinner in the evening. Whaddya' think? Can you send me a letter with a ballpark figure? I've got "The Great Asphincto" booked for a floor show and it promises to be a great evening?? Maybe we can even give it some sort of charity spin??

Big kisses,

Randy!

Randy Lindsay-Bird
Society Secretary

NO REPLY

QUEENS GATE
SCHOOL ROAD, CIRENCESTER
GLOUCESTERSHIRE,
GLX 6DU

The Club Secretary
Edgely Heath Golf Club
Edgely Heath
Gloucestershire
GLB4 9KM

Captain,

22nd April 2007

I'm still in a state of some shock a full month after an incident at your golf course and feel that I must put fingers to keyboard to complain about it. Everything started alright- a pleasant, if windy round with my old friend Colin. We were progressing steadily until we approached the third green (by the canal). There, two "gentlemen," acting like they owned the place, suddenly accosted us. The first one shouted "Sweet and sour pork and chop chop!" while the second started making his eyes go all slitty with his fingers. Being ex Special Forces, I don't shun aggression and asked them what they wanted?

This is where I started to wonder whether someone had dropped something into my breakfast tea? The younger "gentleman" told me that neither he nor his friend (who were both members, or so they said) liked the thought of "Chinky Chonks playing on our course." I was stuck for what to say? I asked him to explain what he meant and the older "gentleman" then jumped in with- "he means that this is not a course where Chinky-Chonks are welcome." Quite apart from the rights and wrongs of this statement, neither Colin nor I could in any way be described as "Chinky Chonks." Colin was born and bred in Guildford whilst I was born in Durham. I still have a faint suntan from my years in the Gulf but could never in a hundred years be taken for a Chinaman.

We told them that we would complain to the club authorities and they just laughed and said that they were all their friends and that they would never listen to a couple of whingeing "Chinky Chonks." We left the course immediately to the sound of the pair making loud "Kung Fu" type noises behind us.

Thinking back on the incident I have several questions. Have I correctly understood the insult? If yes then the whole affair is totally ridiculous and I can send you a photograph of both Colin and myself if required to show you that we are totally British. Does your club have an anti-Chinese policy? Are these "gentlemen" well-known characters at your establishment? They both looked a little like mini-cab drivers: short-cropped hair, earrings, one was wearing a foul-looking canary yellow jumper while the other had badly highlighted hair and a purple "Kangol" polo top. I await your satisfactory response to this matter.

Yours sincerely,

Colonel Arthur.J.Lindsay-Bird (ret)

NO REPLY

Queens Gate,
School Road,
Cirencester,
Gloucestershire,
GLX 6DU

The Club Secretary
████████ Golf Course ████████

28th Feb 2007

Sir,

I am writing to you regarding the forthcoming "Tight Hole World Tour." We're a friendly gay golf society based in ████████, England and eight of our hunkiest members are setting off on a world golf tour in order to raise money for the Cameron Mornay Foundation. The charity intends to raise enough money to allow Cameron, a young protegee of the society to have transgender surgery.

A man called Luis whom I met in Sitges last year, recommended your club and we'd therefore, love to be able to organise the Levantine leg of their tour at your establishment. To qualify as having completed this leg, our members would need to play eighteen holes at your club as four two balls. They would be playing Randy Admiral Rules. You would therefore, obviously need to warn your members of traditions such as the St James' Park Guardsmen or Toad In The Hole. I'm confident that you're a liberal man of the world totally at ease with this kind of thing but one does still find the odd stick in the mud who feels that nudity has no place on the fairway.

Could you let me know what your dress codes are, where the boys could "relax" after the round and whether any of your members would care to join in any social events in the evening? I dimly remember reading about somewhere that you can eat lamb's eyes in tents? Is that the sort of thing they should expect?

We've got loads of money to splash about so just let me know what figure you have in mind and we can start to play ball. Looking forward to your reply.

Yours etc,

Randy!

Randy Lindsay-Bird
Club Secretary

NO REPLY

QUEENS GATE
SCHOOL ROAD, CIRENCESTER
GLOUCESTERSHIRE,
GLX 6DU

The Club Secretary
The Links
Netherly
Wiltshire
TR143 THR

29th May 2007

Sir,

My son David has just gone through an extremely distressing period of psychological problems that forced him to be sectioned under the 1983 Mental Health Act. While "inside" he suffered greatly, finally converting to Islam before returning to work only recently. He has been doing a lot better recently and seems to be on the slow and rocky road to recovery. He works in television and has even won a "TV Quick Award" for his latest project.

You can understand that, as a parent, I want nothing more for him to recover fully (and stop being a Muslim). It is for this reason that I write to you. It has come to my attention that your miniature golf course goes by the alternative and highly offensive moniker of "Crazy Golf." I am most upset by this. How would you feel if you suffered from some terrible disease, as I do, like IBD (Inflammable Bowel Disease) and someone near you decided to change the name of their business to "Ulcerative Colitis Plumbers" or "Abdominal Distention Hardware Store?" You get my point.

I can understand that you have probably never had a relative with psychological problems and have, therefore, never give a thought to the pain that your choice of name can cause others. I ask you to please change the name of your business so that I am not forced to take further action. How about "Eccentric Golf" or maybe "Amusing Golf." Whatever induced you to use the word "Crazy" in the first place is beyond me but it has to stop.

I'm a proper golfer myself and must admit that I do not see the attraction of your "sport" but we live in a country where you can do what you wish. I just ask you to consider the negative effect that it has on those less fortunate than yourselves.

Yours etc

Colonel Arthur Lindsay-Bird (ret)

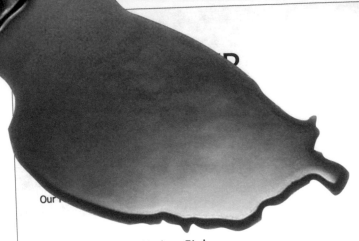

Date: 15th June 2007

Colonel A J Lindsay-Bird
Queens Gate
School Road
Cirencester
Gloucestershire
GLX 6DU

Dear Sir

I thank you for your letter of 29th May 2007 which, having been addressed to ████████████ rather than the Town Council, has only today come into my possession.

I am sorry to hear of your son's circumstances and can reassure you that the naming of the miniature golf course ████████████ was not aimed at your son or anyone who suffers from a mental disorder. The words 'craze' and 'crazy' have a number of meanings, as do many words in the English language.

On reflection I trust that you will appreciate that the Town Council has not acted pejoratively.

Recyclable Paper

Town Council

20th June 2007

Dear Mr ████████

Thank you for your letter in reply to mine outlining my concerns about the use of the name "Crazy Golf." I have to admit to finding your reply quite unsatisfactory. I am well aware that many English words have several meanings- the word "muppet" for instance can denote "a small furry puppet", "a sieved ladle used in Thai cooking" and "an idiot." This, however, does not apply to the usage we are discussing.

Form what I can gather "Crazy Golf" is a pastime whereby people have to putt a golf ball through various odd obstacles such as a windmill, a squiggly hill and, if you can believe it, the mouth of a clown. Why anyone in their right mind would wish to do this is quite beyond me but that is by the by. The point is that the moniker "Crazy" golf is given to it because it is seen as a type of golf designed to appear, at best surreal and at worst the work of a lunatic. I find this very distasteful and demand that the establishment be re-named something like "Mini Golf" or "Different Golf." This would cause no harm to trade and would allow people like my son David to be less of a target for the sneers and jeers of the hoi-polloi.

I will not let this matter rest- I fought in Aden and have a strong backbone. I have already started a petition and will organise a series of demonstrations if I do not receive satisfaction in this matter. This country has already gone far enough awry without having to put up with this sort of blatant offensiveness.

By the way, I knew a Gordon ███████████ in the army. He was with us briefly in Malaya but left under a cloud- something to do with an incident in Panang where he biffed a Chinese chef- any relation?

I await your swift response to this matter.

Yours etc,

Colonel Arthur.J.Lindsay-Bird (ret)

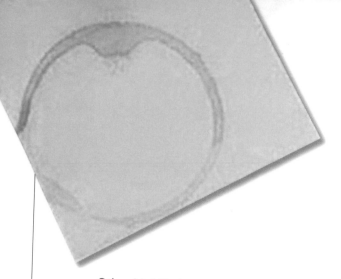

Date: 26th June 2007

Colonel A J Lindsay-Bird
Queens Gate
School Road
Cirencester
Gloucestershire
GLX 6DU

Dear Sir

██████████████████████████

I thank you for your letter of 20th June 2007 and advise you that by the time you receive this letter I shall have handed over the reins as Town Clerk to my successor.

In the circumstances, it would be inappropriate for me to make any further comments on the opening paragraphs of your letter and I will leave it to my successor to consider the way forward.

Your reference to ████████████████ is interesting. Whilst I confirm that to the best of my knowledge and belief he is not a relative, I do understand from my researches that he asked the Chinese chef what his name was and when the chef responded he biffed him. It is perhaps appropriate to mention that the name of the chef was Fuk yu. Perhaps this identifies my point over the peculiarities of language.

Recyclable Paper

NO REPLY